World History

FOCUS
on Economics

Jean Caldwell

James Clark

Walter Herscher

D1452268

National Council
on Economic Education

THE EconomicsAmerica® AND EconomicsInternational® PROGRAMS

AUTHORS

Jean Caldwell
Professor of Economics
University of Central Oklahoma
Edmond, Oklahoma

James Clark
Associate Professor of Economics
Wichita State University
Wichita, Kansas

Walter Herscher
Secondary Social Studies Department Head
Appleton Area School District
Appleton, Wisconsin

with assistance from

Mark C. Schug
Professor of Curriculum and Instruction
University of Wisconsin, Milwaukee

REVIEWERS

Loy Bilderback
Professor of History
California State University, Fresno

Don Leet
Professor of Economics
California State University, Fresno

Robert Catus
Arsenal Technical High School
Indianapolis, Indiana

Sally G. Finch
The Westminster Schools
Atlanta, Georgia

Robert Fulmer
Trinity Preparatory School
Winter Park, Florida

FIELD TEST TEACHERS

Pam Branham
Edmond Memorial High School
Edmond, Oklahoma

Charles Ekrut
Wichita Southeast High School
Wichita, Kansas

Mary Lindgren
Armstrong Senior High School
Neenah, Wisconsin

John Roberson
Broken Arrow High School
Broken Arrow, Oklahoma

Jana Roth
Broken Arrow High School
Broken Arrow, Oklahoma

Connie Schillingburg
Edmond Memorial High School
Edmond, Oklahoma

Third Printing, 2001. Second Printing, 1998. Copyright © 1996, National Council on Economic Education, 1140 Avenue of the Americas, New York, NY 10036. All rights reserved. The activities and worksheets may be duplicated for classroom use, the number not to exceed the number of students in each class. Notice of copyright must appear on all pages. With the exception of the activities and worksheets, no part of this book may be reproduced in any form or by any means without permission in writing from the publisher. Printed in the United States of America.

ISBN 1-56183-490-4

5 4 3

CONTENTS

FOREWORD

World History: Focus on Economics, a core volume in a new generation of National Council publications is dedicated to increasing the economic literacy of *all* students. The Focus publications, the new centerpiece of **Economics**America, build on almost five decades of success in delivering economic education to America's students.

The *Focus* series is both new and innovative, using economics primarily to enhance learning in such classes as history, geography, civics, and personal finance, as well as in economics classes. Activities are interactive, reflecting the belief that students learn best through active, highly personalized experiences with economics. Applications of economic understanding to real world situations and contexts dominate the lessons. In addition, the lessons explicitly teach the voluntary national standards in economics, outlined in the National Council's *A Framework for Teaching Basic Economic Concepts.*

World History: Focus on Economics opens with an exploration of the first economic revolution, setting the stage for the dramatic unfolding of the role economics has played in world history. The lessons that follow focus on two topics: why did some economies grow and prosper while others remained stagnant or declined; and what causes people to make choices that help or hinder economic growth. Students discover that, from an economic standpoint, the history of the world is the history of people and nations making decisions about how to use scarce resources. They unravel such mysteries as how the Black Death raised living standards in Europe, why China didn't discover the New World, and why the industrial revolution started in England. Easily understood economic principles surface repeatedly in different contexts to help explain economic history and people's roles in the economy.

Michael Watts, Professor of Economics, Purdue University, and Senior Fellow, National Council on Economic Education, reviewed the manuscript and offered many valuable suggestions. The authors and the publisher are responsible for the final publication.

The National Council thanks the chief author, Jean Caldwell, Professor of Economics at the University of Oklahoma; and coauthors, James Clark, Associate Professor of Economics at Wichita State University; and Walter Herscher, Secondary Social Studies Department Head in the Appleton, Wisconsin, Area School District. We recognize, as well, the financial support of the National Science Foundation.

Robert F. Duvall, President & CEO
National Council on Economic Education

INTRODUCTION

The history of the people and nations who have inhabited this world for the past 10,000 years can be studied from many different points of view. Students can learn about rulers and governmental institutions, wars and transfers of power. They can study the philosophies and beliefs that influenced people in different regions of the world at different time periods. They can look at how geography shaped the ways that people lived, or how art, music, drama, and architecture reflected and influenced the cultures that produced them.

World History: Focus on Economics looks at the economic aspects of world history: How did people satisfy their material wants in various places and times? What forces caused prosperity to increase in some nations while it declined in others?

ECONOMICS AND WORLD HISTORY

The basic insight that economics brings to history is that no society can have all of the material goods and services that its people would like to have. There are not enough productive resources— natural resources, labor, or capital goods— to satisfy all the wants of a society. From an economic standpoint, the history of the world is the history of people and nations making decisions about how to use their scarce resources.

Most of the lessons in *World History: Focus on Economics* address one of two major topics:

- Why do some economies grow and prosper while others remain stagnant or decline?
- What causes people to make choices that help or hinder economic growth?

ECONOMIC GROWTH AND PRODUCTIVITY

Fundamental to economic growth is increasing *productivity*. Productivity is most commonly defined as the amount of output produced by a worker over a certain period of time, such as a day, a month, or a year. (Productivity can also be measured as output of land or of some other resource.) Most of the increases in the material wealth and improved living standards of the various societies of the world can be attributed to increases in productivity. What causes productivity to increase? Some of the

factors that economists agree are important are:

- More and better capital goods
- Specialization and division of labor
- Improved technology
- Education and training
- Improved transportation

Productivity is specifically taught in Lesson Two, "Making Clothes and Houses Out of Wheat," Lesson Ten, "How the Industrial Revolution Raised Living Standards," and Lesson Eleven, "Japan's Economic Miracle." Lesson Three, "Trade in Africa, 9th to 12th Centuries A.D.," focuses primarily on transportation.

ECONOMIC GROWTH AND INCENTIVE STRUCTURES

Economic historians are increasingly emphasizing the role of incentives in economic growth and productivity increases. Lesson Five, "Why Didn't China Discover the New World?," and Lesson Six, "The Decline of Spain," give examples of how the incentives in each of these societies hindered long-term economic growth. Lesson Four, "How Did the Black Death Raise Living Standards in Europe?," shows how the incentives to landowners changed after the Black Death drastically reduced the number of peasants on whose labor the landlords depended. Lesson Eight, "Adam Smith and the Market Economy," illustrates how free markets provide incentives for producers to serve the interests of consumers. Lesson Nine, "The Industrial Revolution," contrasts the incentives to invention and innovation that existed in France and in England in the eighteenth century. Lesson Twelve, "The Fall of Communism," contrasts the incentives present in command institutions with those of market institutions.

Lesson Seven, "The Great Tulip Boom," provides an occasion for students to learn about the relationship between risk and reward, a very important concept in the area of personal investment.

UNDERSTANDING CHOICES IN HISTORY

Economics tends to view people as rational choice makers, rather than as helpless victims of circumstance. Lesson One, "The First Economic Revolution," introduces four principles that are used throughout the lessons to analyze the choices that people made at various points in history:

- People choose.
- People's choices involve costs.
- People respond to incentives in predictable ways.
- People's choices have consequences that lie in the future.

These principles of economic reasoning can be applied, not only to the past, but also to present decisions that students must make. A major goal of this publication is to provide students with practice in analyzing decisions that they can use in their own lives.

The four principles given above are a reduced version of the decision-making model presented in *United States History: Eyes on the Economy*, published by the National Council on Economic Education. Also borrowed from *Eyes on the Economy* is the device of the "mystery" given at the beginning of each lesson. The purpose of each mystery is to present a problem that can be analyzed by applying principles of economic reasoning. Possible ways to use the mysteries are as an advance organizer (either read or displayed on a visual), an item for small group discussion, or an essay test question. (The mystery approach is used in *Capstone: The Nation's High School Economics Course*, also published by NCEE.)

The authors of *World History: Focus on Economics* have provided lessons that actively involve students in the learning process. Several lessons include simulations, and many provide small group activities. Each lesson can be completed in one class period, although closure and assessment activities may extend into a second period. Sample multiple-choice and essay test items for each lesson are at the end of the book.

The authors hope that you and your students enjoy these lessons and come away with a deeper understanding of history and of the human beings who made it.

ABILITY GUIDELINES AND FLEXIBILITY OF TEXT

World History: Focus on Economics is suitable for a wide variety of curriculum needs and teaching strategies. The program allows for great flexibility in teaching and learning—offering ample support for students of different ability levels. As there is no single approach or method adequate in all situations, the authors suggest many approaches for teachers to choose from to best suit the needs of their individual courses and to match the abilities, interests, and backgrounds of students. In general, the lessons are for all students.

KEY TO ABILITY LEVELS

The following coding system identifies activities suitable for students of various ability levels:

★ all students—basic course material
■ average and above average students

PLANNING CHART

Shown here are lesson summaries to help in planning.

LESSON	CONCEPTS	SUMMARY	MATERIALS NEEDED
1. The First Economic Revolution	Choices, Costs, Incentives	Students learn to use four basic principles of economic reasoning to understand why some nomadic groups may have shifted to a settled agricultural lifestyle.	Copies of Activities 1, 2, and 3
2. Making Clothes and Houses Out of Wheat	Productivity, Capital Goods, Consumer Goods, Standard of Living	Students perform a simulation that shows how increases in agricultural productivity allowed Neolithic farming cultures to raise their living standards.	Game pieces made from Activities 1 and 2, copies of Activities 3 and 4
3. Trade in Africa in the 9th to 12th Centuries A.D.	Incentives, Trade, Profit, Transportation Cost	Students calculate the efficiency of several alternative forms of transportation in 12th Century Africa in terms of load carried, miles traveled, and cost, in order to study decision making by North African traders.	Transparency of Visual 1, copies of Activities 1, 2, and 3
4. How Did the Black Death Raise Living Standards in Europe?	Choices, Incentives, Production Costs, Profits, Trade	Students calculate the costs and decisions of an English landlord before and after the Black Death.	Transparency of Visual 1, copies of Activities 1 and 2
5. Why Didn't China Discover the New World?	Economic Growth, Technology, Trade, Incentives	Students in small groups discuss why superior Chinese naval technology did not result in significant exploration and trade.	Transparency of Visual 1 and copies of Activity 1

LESSON	CONCEPTS	SUMMARY	MATERIALS NEEDED
6. The Decline of Spain	Economic Growth, Government Spending, Taxation, Monopoly, Human Resources, Inflation	Students work in groups to study the Spanish economy of the 16th century and draw conclusions for developing nations today.	Transparency of Visual 1, copies of Activities 1, 2, 3, and 4
7. The Great Tulip Boom	Financial Investment, Rate of Return, Risk, Speculation	Students perform a simulation of the tulip bulb market in 17th century Netherlands in order to understand the role of speculation in economic booms.	Transparency of Visual 1, marking pen, envelopes, game pieces made from Activity 1, copies of Activity 2
8. Adam Smith and the Market Economy	Self-Interest, Competition, Government Regulation, Monopolies, Market Economy, Investor	Students perform a simulation that illustrates how self-interest causes merchants and investors to behave in ways that benefit society.	Copies of Activities 1, 2, 3, and 5, ballots made from Activity 4
9. The Industrial Revolution	Incentives, Profit, Innovation, Economic Growth	Students in small groups decide whether each of a number of characteristics of French and of British society in the 1800s had a positive or negative effect on economic growth.	Transparency of Visual 1, copies of Activities 1 and 2
10. How the Industrial Revolution Raised Living Standards	Productivity, Unit Costs, Specialization and Division of Labor, Capital Goods. Technology, Transportation Costs, Standard of Living	Students perform a simulation that illustrates division of labor and improved capital goods and study and discuss a reading on Josiah Wedgwood. The reading illustrates those and other causes of productivity.	Three scissors, four red crayons, transparency of Visual 1, and copies of Activities 1 and 2

LESSON	CONCEPTS	SUMMARY	MATERIALS NEEDED
11. Japan's Economic Miracle	Economic Growth, Productivity, Capital, Human Capital, Interest Rates	Students in small groups discuss factors contributing to Japan's economic growth after World War II.	Transparency of Visual 1, copies of Activities 1 and 2
12. The Fall of Communism	Economic Systems, Command Economy, Market Economy, Incentives	Students read two accounts written by a U.S. high school teacher about her 1987 trip through the then Soviet Union and discuss what her experiences reveal about incentives in a command economy.	Copies of Activities 1, 2, and 3

LESSON ONE
THE FIRST ECONOMIC REVOLUTION

INTRODUCTION

History There have been human beings on earth for more than a million years. However, most of the major advances of the human race have been compressed into the past 10,000 years. It was about 10,000 years ago, at the dawn of the neolithic period, that many hunter/gatherer societies developed a settled agricultural lifestyle.

Mystery Many scholars believe that the nomadic hunting/gathering groups of 10,000 years ago could normally get all the food they wanted without working as hard as the first farming people worked. Why would people choose to be farmers if they had to work harder than they had before?

Economic History Economists think of human beings as basically rational creatures who make choices based upon expected costs and benefits. To those nomadic peoples who settled into an agricultural way of life, the benefits of a more regular and dependable source of food probably outweighed the cost of harder work and perhaps a more monotonous diet.

CONCEPTS
Choices
Costs
Incentives

OBJECTIVE
◆ Learn and apply four basic principles of economic reasoning

LESSON DESCRIPTION
The teacher explains four basic principles of economic reasoning, using a modern example. Students in groups then apply the same principles to understanding why some nomadic hunting/gathering groups may have shifted to a settled agricultural lifestyle and what the consequences of their choice were.

TIME REQUIRED
One class period

MATERIALS
★One copy for each student of Activities 1, 2, and 3

PROCEDURE
1. Explain that in Southern California some young people spend most of every day surfing rather than going to school or to work. In some ways, it's a wonderful life—sunshine, fresh air, and the thrill of searching for the perfect wave. They don't need many clothes or much money. There are no bosses to order them around.

2. Ask students to imagine two eighteen-year-olds, Joe and Jeff. Joe is a surfer who spends almost every day at the beach. Occasionally he works at a part-time job to get enough money to eat and to buy wax for his surfboard. Jeff likes to surf, too, but his opportunities to do so are limited because he has a full-time job as the assistant manager at a fast-food restaurant.

3. Ask students what the advantages of Joe's surfer lifestyle are? (Time to enjoy a sport he loves, fresh air and sunshine, no boss to order him around.) What are the disadvantages? (Low income and little ability to buy desirable goods and services.) What are the advantages and disadvantages of Joe's lifestyle as a full-time worker? (Joe has more income, but his time is not his own and he is giving up leisure.)

4. Tell students that human beings throughout history have had to make choices about how to live their lives. We can understand history better if we know how and why people make the choices that they do.

5. Distribute Activity 1. Explain that these principles of economic reasoning can be used to understand choices that people make today and have made in the past. Explain the four principles and apply them to the choice of being a full-time surfer or a full-time worker.

People Choose. Explain that, although individuals often say, "I did so-and-so because

I had no choice," usually there are alternatives among which they can choose. Some young people actually choose to spend most of every day surfing, at least for a few years. More young people choose to work full-time or to go to school.

People's Choices Involve Costs. Explain that, when individuals choose one alternative, they give up other alternatives that may also have some advantages. What does Joe have to give up? (The income to buy many desirable goods and services; the opportunity to establish a work record and learn saleable skills.) What does Jeff have to give up? (Leisure time and some control over his actions.)

People Respond to Incentives in Predictable Ways. Explain that an incentive is something that encourages an individual to choose a particular alternative. What incentives are there to be a full-time surfer? (Time to enjoy the beach and to perfect surfing skill.) What incentives are there to be the assistant manager at a fast-food restaurant? (A regular source of income, ability to buy more goods and services, an employment record, chance to learn saleable skills.)

People's Choices Have Consequences That Lie in the Future. Explain that one cannot always know what all the consequences of a choice may be. Ask students what some long-term consequences might be of choosing to be a full-time surfer or the assistant manager of a fast-food restaurant? (Answers will vary. If Joe later decides to get a job, he has missed an opportunity to build up a good work record and valuable job skills. On the other hand, Jeff might in later years look back with regret on his lost opportunities to improve his surfing skills and to enjoy leisure time at the beach.)

6. Explain that some of the people who lived at the beginning of the Neolithic period faced a choice similar to the choice of being a surfer or a worker. Many scholars believe that the first people to become settled farmers may have chosen a

lifestyle that involved harder work than the way of life they were giving up—that of being nomadic hunter/gatherers. Why would people make a choice that involved harder work? Suggest to students that the same principles of economic reasoning might be used to explain the decision of these people.

7. Divide students into small groups. Give each student a copy of Activities 2 and 3. Have the groups read Activity 2 and also the part of their world history textbook that discusses the first farming peoples. (Every textbook probably covers this. However, you may also wish to find some additional reading material on this topic.) Then have each group discuss and write down answers to Activity 3. Suggested answers are:

1. They chose to settle in one place and to become farmers.

2. The quantity of food available is probably more reliable, and it is easier to store food for bad times if one is in a settled village. People might also have responded to a change in the availability of food by hunting fewer large animals or having fewer children.

3. Some leisure, according to the scholars quoted in Activity 2.

4. Settled agriculture ultimately allowed more food to be produced than growers needed. This freed some workers to specialize in producing other kinds of goods and services. (This point is illustrated by the simulation in Lesson 2.) Some agricultural villages grew to be true cities.

CLOSURE

Review the answers of the small groups in class. Stress the point that historical events are the result of human choices. Also point out that historical events can help people understand current issues and problems. This idea is central to economic reasoning about the past.

ACTIVITY 1
SOME PRINCIPLES OF ECONOMIC REASONING

Name _____

1. People choose.

2. People's choices involve costs.

3. People respond to incentives in predictable ways.

4. People's choices have consequences that lie in the future.

ACTIVITY 2
WHICH WOULD YOU RATHER BE, A NOMADIC HUNTER/GATHERER OR A FARMER?

Name _____

Why did some groups of people in various areas of the world abandon hunting animals and gathering wild foods as a way of life in order to become farmers? The nomadic hunters and gatherers of Paleolithic times are often pictured as struggling desperately to find enough food to survive. When some hunting/gathering bands began to plant and harvest crops, domesticate animals, and live in permanent settlements, their lives improved dramatically, according to this view.

However, a number of anthropologists who study present-day hunting/gathering societies, have challenged this interpretation. Richard Lee, for example, estimated that women of the !Kung tribe of Africa could gather enough food in six hours to feed their families for three days, while even the most ambitious man of the tribe averaged less than 32 hours a week hunting. Reasoning from this and other studies, anthropologist Marshall Sahlins concluded that many Paleolithic hunter/gatherers may have lived relatively easy lives.

On the other hand, the earliest people who turned to settled agriculture probably worked very hard. They had to dig and turn soil in order to make the earth more receptive to seeds. They had to keep weeds out of the field. If men gave up hunting in order to farm, there would be less meat available to eat. Women would not be able to gather as wide a variety of nuts, berries, and other plants. Why would people shift to a lifestyle that involved harder work and a less varied diet?

Information taken from Richard B. Lee and Irven Devore (eds.), *Man the Hunter*, Chicago: Aldine, Atherton, 1972.

ACTIVITY 3

Name _____

1. What choice did some nomadic hunter/gatherer bands make?

2. What incentives might there be for a group of hunter/gatherers to become farmers?

3. What would the costs be to hunter/gatherers of becoming farmers?

4. Over a long period of time, what were the consequences of this choice?

LESSON TWO
MAKING CLOTHES AND HOUSES OUT OF WHEAT

INTRODUCTION

History Ten thousand years ago, settled agriculture developed in the Middle East, based on planting grain and on breeding and herding animals. As agricultural tools improved, humans were able to increase the amount of food they could produce and thus could take time away from raising crops to raise their standard of living by making better clothes, houses, and many other things.

Mystery How can raising more wheat help people to get better clothes and houses?

Economic History To "increase productivity" means to increase the output of productive resources such as a worker over a given period of time, such as an hour, a day, or a year. When early farming people increased their agriculture productivity, less labor was required to produce food, freeing some labor for use in producing other goods or services. The development of better tools was one way in which agriculture became more productive.

CONCEPTS
Productivity
Capital Goods
Consumer Goods
Standard of Living

OBJECTIVES
◆ Analyze the relationship of capital goods to productivity

◆ Analyze the relationship between productivity and the total amount of goods and services available to a society

◆ Recognize that a surplus of agricultural products frees resources that can then be used in the production of other goods and services

LESSON DESCRIPTION
Students participate in a simulation about an agricultural village in Neolithic times. The teacher debriefs the simulation, emphasizing relevant economic concepts.

TIME REQUIRED
One or two class periods

MATERIALS
★ Sufficient game pieces made from Activities 1 and 2 that, for each group, there are:
10   1-unit wheat pieces
10   5-unit wheat pieces
10   10-unit wheat pieces
 9   hoes
 9   sickles
 1   canal system
10   garments
 1   mud-brick house
 1   copy of Activities 3 and 4 for each student

PROCEDURE
1. Explain that one of the most important topics in world history is how people have raised their *standard of living* over time. Ask students what the term "standard of living" means. (An increase in the average quantity and quality of goods and services available to people in a society.) Ask students how the standard of living in the United States today is different from what it was a hundred years ago. (More and higher quality food, better housing, better health care, and so on.) Explain that today students are going to take part in a simulation that shows how the standard of living increased in agricultural villages of the Neolithic period.

2. Use the following simulation to illustrate how increases in productivity led to a higher standard of living among early agricultural peoples:

A. Select one student to serve as a "clerk" to help you conduct the simulation. Divide the remainder of the class into no more than four groups. (A small number of groups makes the simulation faster and easier to operate.) Explain to students that each group represents a family of Neolithic villagers who lived in the Middle East about 8,000 years ago. Tell them, "Your family raises wheat, which is cooked into a thick gruel or baked into unleavened loaves. The only tools that you have are fire-hardened wooden digging sticks that you use to make holes in the ground into which kernels of wheat are placed and covered with dirt. You also raise sheep, which you use for meat. You do not make woolen cloth, but a band of hunters from your village recently visited another village and brought back a woolen garment. Your family thinks that such garments would be more comfortable than the animal skins you now wear, and would also be easier to make."

B. Give each family enough copies of Activity 3 for each group member. Explain "The goal of each group in this simulation is to raise its standard of living. Each year, each family member needs 20 units of wheat for an adequate level of nutrition. The simulation will end when one or more families has 20 units of wheat, 10 woolen garments, and a sturdy mud-brick house to replace the uncomfortable and fragile mud hut in which they currently live."

Further explain, "It takes time to shear sheep, make wool into thread, weave cloth, and sew garments together. Therefore, each woolen garment will cost your family two units of wheat. Those two units represent wheat that was given up because someone's labor was used to make a garment instead of to plant, cultivate and harvest wheat. It also takes time to form mud into bricks, lay the bricks out in the sun to bake, and then to build a house. A mud-brick house will cost your family 20 units of wheat."

C. Tell the clerk to give each family 30 units of wheat. Explain to students, "In a normal year, your family can produce 20 units of wheat, which is enough to feed you comfortably through the year. This year, the weather has been exceptionally good and you have 30 units of wheat. Over the coming year, your family will consume

20 units of wheat. You will have 10 units left over. You can choose to store these units, in case there is a drought next year, or you can exchange some of the excess units for clothing or for hoes, sickles, or a system of irrigation canals."

Explain further, "In order to have enough units of wheat to obtain woolen garments and a mud-brick house, you must find a way to increase the amount of wheat you produce. You could produce more wheat if your family had hoes to keep weeds out of your field, or sickles to allow you to harvest more quickly. But to make these tools, time must be given up that could have been spent in the fields. Therefore, each hoe costs three units of wheat, and each sickle costs two units of wheat. Your family lives near a river and could dig canals to your fields to increase the amount of water for your crops. Initially, digging these canals would be quite time-consuming, however, so the cost is 20 units. You may choose to cooperate with another family to build a more extensive canal system. In this case, the total cost will be 30 units (15 for each family)."

D. Give each family enough copies of Activity 4 for each group member. Explain, "Each round of this simulation is a year. The simulation will end in any year in which one or more families has 20 units of wheat, 10 woolen garments, and a mud-brick house. Notice that you don't win this simulation by accumulating a certain number of hoes and sickles, or by building canals. Hoes, sickles, and irrigation canals are examples of *capital goods.* Capital goods are goods that are used to produce other goods or services. Hoes, sickles, and irrigation canals help you to produce more wheat, which gives your family more time to weave cloth and to build a house. Wheat, clothes, and houses are *Consumer goods,* goods that give you direct satisfaction. You can't eat, wear, or live in the capital goods you acquire in this game, but you can use them to obtain the consumer goods that raise your standard of living."

E. Begin the simulation by instructing each family to decide how many units of wheat to store and how many to exchange for hoes and sickles. Remind them that at the end of the year they must turn in 20 units to the clerk, which represent the amount of wheat they consume during the year.

F. Call on a representative of each family in turn to exchange wheat with the clerk for hoes and sickles. At the same time, they should turn in 20 units of wheat for consumption.

G. Call on a representative of each family to collect next year's crop from the clerk. Each family should receive 20 units of wheat plus any additional wheat they are entitled to because of the capital goods they own.

H. Continue the above procedure in subsequent years (rounds). At the beginning of the fourth year, before each family purchases capital goods, announce that a drought has occurred. Collect 10 units of wheat from each family. (If you are using this simulation with more than one class, vary the year in which the drought occurs.) Remind students that, at the end of the year (round), each family must have 20 units of wheat to consume (turn in to the clerk) or it will be considered dead.

Family representatives may buy a canal system in any round at the same time they buy hoes and sickles. They may buy woolen garments or a mud-brick house in any round at the same time they "consume" units of wheat, or they may save units of wheat until they have enough to buy all the consumer goods they need to win the simulation.

3. Debrief the simulation, using the following outline:

A. Write the word *productivity* on the chalkboard. Tell students that productivity is the output of goods or services that a worker (or group of workers) produces in a given time period, such as an hour, a day, or a year. Remind students that each family started the simulation with 30 units of wheat. Ask each family how much their productivity increased by the end of the simulation. (The difference between 30 units and the number of units they produced in the last round.)

B. Ask students what caused the increases in productivity during the simulation. (More tools and possibly the use of a canal system.) Remind students that tools and canals are both examples of capital goods. Capital goods are human-made goods that are used to produce other goods or services. The use of more and better capital goods has improved productivity throughout history.

C. In order to get tools and canals, families had to give up something. What did they give up? (Units of wheat.)

D. At the beginning of the simulation, were families able to obtain woolen garments or a mud brick house? (No, because they would have had to have given up so much wheat that they might have endangered their survival.) Explain that, as long as most people in a society have to spend most or all of their time to produce enough food to survive, there is little available labor to produce other goods and services. The existence of an agricultural surplus is necessary before a society can begin to produce a wide variety of goods and services.

CLOSURE

Explain that, 5,000 years after the time in which their simulation took place, large cities flourished in the region of Sumer (today, southern Iraq). Workers included scribes, merchants, metalsmiths, and potters, as well as priests and government officials. What does this wide variety of nonfarming workers imply about agricultural productivity? (Productivity must have increased greatly over the 5,000 year period in order for the economy to be able to support so many nonfarming workers.)

ACTIVITY 1

Name _____

1 Unit of Wheat	1 Unit of Wheat	1 Unit of Wheat	1 Unit of Wheat	1 Unit of Wheat
5 Units of Wheat	5 Units of Wheat	5 Units of Wheat	5 Units of Wheat	5 Units of Wheat
10 Units of Wheat	10 Units of Wheat	10 Units of Wheat	10 Units of Wheat	10 Units of Wheat

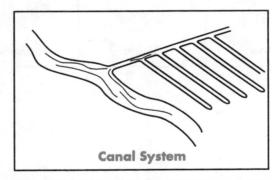

Canal System

Mud-brick House

ACTIVITY 2

Name _____

 **Woolen Garment**  **Woolen Garment** **Woolen Garment** **Woolen Garment** **Woolen Garment**

 **Hoe**  **Hoe**  **Hoe**  **Hoe**  **Hoe**

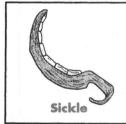 **Sickle**  **Sickle**  **Sickle**  **Sickle** 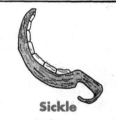 **Sickle**

 From *World History: Focus on Economics,* © National Council on Economic Education, New York, NY

ACTIVITY 3

Name_____

GOALS FOR YOUR FAMILY

- 20 units of wheat each year

- 10 woolen garments (cost of 1 garment = 2 units of wheat)

- 1 mud-brick house (cost = 20 units of wheat)

COST OF CAPITAL GOODS

- 1 hoe = 3 units of wheat (will add 9 units to production each year)

- 1 sickle = 2 units of wheat (will add 5 units to production each year)

- 1 canal system = 20 units (will add 20 units to production each year; if two families cooperate, the cost is 15 units per family, and each family will increase production by 20 units)

ACTIVITY 4
INSTRUCTIONS FOR EACH FAMILY

Name _____

1. In Year 1, decide how many units of wheat you will store against possible future drought. Send a family representative to the clerk to turn in 20 units of wheat, which represents the consumption of your family. He or she should then buy the hoes and sickles your family has decided to purchase.

2. In each subsequent year, the teacher will call a representative of each family in turn to go to the clerk to collect their year's crop of wheat. The family representative will receive 20 units of wheat, PLUS an additional 5 units of wheat for each sickle owned by the family and an additional nine units of wheat for each hoe owned by the family. The family representative must show each hoe and sickle to the clerk at the time he or she collects units of wheat. If the family acquires a canal system, they may collect an additional 20 units.

Note: No family may own more than 9 hoes, 9 sickles, or 1 canal system.

3. After all families have collected their wheat, the teacher will call a representative of each family to turn in 20 units of wheat to the clerk, representing the amount of wheat the family consumes in that year. The representative may also exchange units of wheat for clothing or for a mud-brick house at this time.

4. A drought may occur in any year. When it does, each family will have to turn in 10 additional units of wheat to the clerk. A family that does not have 20 units to consume after they have turned in 10 units to the clerk will die.

The simulation ends in the round (year) in which one or more families possesses 20 units of wheat, 10 woolen garments, and a mud-brick house.

LESSON THREE
TRADE IN AFRICA 9TH TO 12TH CENTURIES A.D.

INTRODUCTION

History Long before Europeans made contact with the African continent, long-distance trade flourished in Africa. North African camel caravans made long and dangerous journeys across the Sahara to trade with the West Africans.

Mystery Traveling from North Africa to West Africa involved many dangers and hardships. Why would people voluntarily make this journey?

Economic Reasoning The people of West Africa wanted salt for their diets to replace the salt that they lost through perspiration in the hot climate. But there was little salt available in West Africa. Because salt could be mined in North Africa, and because the kingdom of Ghana in West Africa produced a great deal of gold, an opportunity for trade existed. The profit to be made in trading salt and other goods for gold provided the North Africans with an incentive to undertake the long and hazardous journey.

CONCEPTS
Incentives
Trade
Profit
Transportation Cost

OBJECTIVES
◆ Identify profit as an incentive to undertake trade over long distances

◆ Understand that transportation costs must be covered in order for long-distance trade to be profitable

◆ Calculate the total output, in terms of cargo capacity and miles covered, of alternative methods of transportation

LESSON DESCRIPTION
The teacher displays a visual showing the geographic regions and trade routes between North and West Africa. Students read a short passage and answer questions in class discussion. Students in groups calculate the efficiency of various methods of transportation available to the traders who carried goods between North and West Africa. They next calculate costs of several methods of transportation, and finally analyze why traders sometimes had to use less efficient or more costly kinds of transportation.

TIME REQUIRED
One class period

MATERIALS
1 transparency of Visual 1
★ 1 copy of Activities 1, 2, and 3 for each student

PROCEDURE
1. Explain that trade among different societies helps human beings raise their living standards. In any society, there are many goods that cannot be produced locally or can be produced only at a relatively high cost. The people in a society benefit when they can trade goods that are abundant or easily produced in their society to other peoples, and receive in return goods that would be relatively costly if produced in their own society.

2. Explain that trade across the Sahara Desert flourished from the 9th to the 12th centuries A.D. Camel caravans from North Africa carried many trade goods across the desert to exchange for gold produced in the kingdom of Ghana. Display Visual 1, "Trade Routes in West Africa." Tell students that one of the most important goods traded was salt. There was little salt available in the savanna and rain forest areas and people who lived in those areas wanted to add salt to their diets to replenish the salt they lost through perspiration. Traders from North Africa found it profitable to transport slabs of rock salt weighing from 25 to 40 kilograms across the desert.

3. Distribute Activity 1, "Trade in Africa, 9th to 12th Centuries A.D.," to each student and ask students to read it. After students have read Activity 1, ask them the following questions:

A. The trade between people who lived in North Africa and those who lived in West Africa was very difficult to carry out and involved many dangers. What incentive was there for people to become involved in this trade? (Answer: Hope of making a profit.)

B. Because of the trading expeditions, rock salt was for sale both in North Africa and in West Africa. Do you think that the price of rock salt was the same in West Africa as it was in North Africa? Why or why not? (Answer: The price would probably have been higher in West Africa because the costs of travel would have to be included in the price. Traders would normally not carry rock salt to West Africa unless they expected to cover all their costs, including transportation costs.)

C. Explain that there were many forms of transportation available to traders as they made their way from North Africa to West Africa. If you were a trader, what things would you consider in choosing how to transport your goods? (Answer: Pounds carried, time required, and other factors affecting cost.)

4. Distribute Activity 2, "Transportation Alternatives," to each student. Explain that several different alternatives were available to traders who transported goods to the savanna and rain forest areas of West Africa. Two of the factors that traders considered were how many pounds of cargo could be transported by each type of carrier, and how fast each type of carrier could travel. Tell students that, in order to compare the efficiency of the various transportation choices available to the traders, they must determine the method of transportation that could carry the greatest number of pounds the farthest distance per day. (The figures on how much could be carried and how many miles a day could be covered, are approximated, using a number of sources and, in many cases, averaging estimates made by several authors.)

Divide students into pairs or small groups and ask them to calculate the "pound miles" of each form of transportation by multiplying the pounds that could be carried by the number of miles that could be covered in a day. (Answers: camel, 10,000; canoe, per paddler, 19,000; donkey, 2,000; Human head-loader, 1,200; ox, 4,000; ox cart, 12,000.)

When the students have finished, ask them which kind of transportation carries the greatest amount of cargo farthest in a day? (Canoes.) Ask them to refer back to Activity 1 and tell why they think that canoes were not used in any stage of the trade journey. (There were no rivers in the desert. South of the Sahara, rivers were sometimes flooded and sometimes too shallow to navigate. Many had dangerous rapids.) What method yields the second greatest output? (Ox carts.) Ask them to decide why they think ox carts were not used for any stage of the journey from North Africa through the savanna and the rain forest? (In the desert, there was not enough water for oxen, and carts would have bogged down in the sand. South of the Sahara, roads were unpaved and in poor condition. In the rain forest, oxen might fall victim to the tsetse fly. Human carriers might also be bitten by tsetse flies, but they were hired by the day and could presumably be replaced at little expense.)

5. Distribute Activity 3 to student groups and ask them to calculate the costs of transporting 8,000 pounds of goods 500 miles, using a camel caravan, a donkey caravan, or a caravan of human carriers. Remind them that pounds carried and miles per day are given on Activity 1. Answers are given below:

Camel Caravan:
8,000 pounds would require 20 camels, each carrying 400 lbs.

Traveling 500 miles at 25 miles a day would take 20 days.

20 camels would require 5 drivers, each in charge of 4 camels.

20 camels, each selling for $5, would cost $100.

Wages of 7 cents each for 5 drivers for 20 days would cost $7.

Total cost would be $107.

Donkey Caravan:
8,000 pounds would require 80 donkeys, each carrying 100 lbs.

Traveling 500 miles at 20 miles a day would take 25 days.

80 donkeys would require 16 drivers.

80 donkeys would cost $80.

Wages of 7 cents each for 16 drivers for 25 days would cost $28.

Total cost would be $108.

Human Caravan:
(cargo loaded on heads)
8,000 pounds would require 133 carriers, each carrying 60 lbs.

Traveling 500 miles at 20 miles a day would take 25 days.

Wages of 7 cents each for carrier for 25 days would cost $232.75.

6. Ask students why traders used the most expensive transportation method, human carriers, to travel through the rain forest. (Camels and donkeys would be at risk of being bitten by tsetse flies. The traders assumed no risk of death with human carriers, who were not owned, but employed by the day.)

CLOSURE

Explain that people living in West Africa today still want salt in their diets. Ask students how they think salt is imported into West Africa today. (Probably by oceangoing ships or in trucks driven over improved roads.) Ask how this probably affects the price of salt. (Salt is probably cheaper because it does not cost so much to transport.) Explain that when more pounds can be transported more quickly, transportation costs are likely to be lower and therefore goods can be sold more cheaply.

VISUAL 1
AFRICAN TRADE IN THE 12TH CENTURY

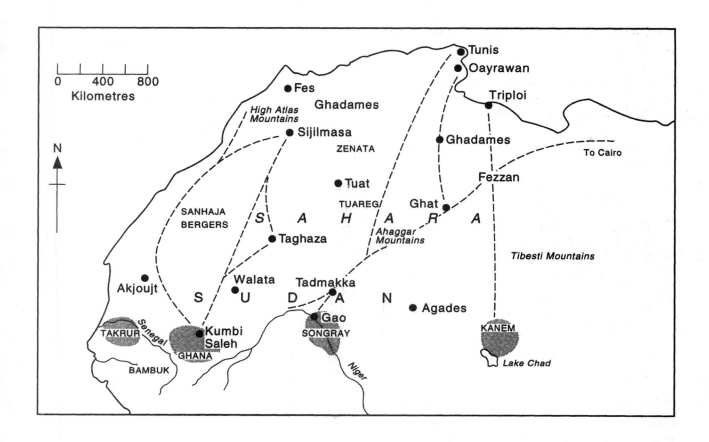

ACTIVITY 1
TRADE IN AFRICA, 9TH TO 12TH CENTURIES A.D.

Name _____

Traders who traveled from North Africa across the Sahara Desert to the savanna and rain forest areas of West Africa experienced many dangers and difficulties. The Sahara extends about 1,800 kilometers from north to south. There were no marked routes and few oases where water could be obtained. Daytime temperatures could rise to 120° or 130° in summer. Sandstorms were frequent.

South of the Sahara, roads were unpaved and in poor condition. Rivers were unpredictable, with water rising to flood conditions at some times or becoming too shallow to navigate in dry periods. Many rivers had dangerous rapids. In the rain forest area, the tsetse fly spread sleeping sickness, which was usually fatal to people and animals.

Trading expeditions originating in North Africa transported goods by camel caravan to the south edge of the Sahara. There the goods were loaded on oxen or donkeys for the trip across the savanna. When trade goods were transported from the savanna to the rain forest, they were once again unloaded and transferred to human carriers, who transported the goods on their heads.

ACTIVITY 2
TRANSPORTATION ALTERNATIVES

Name _____

METHOD OF TRANSPORTATION	CARGO CAPACITY (POUNDS)	MILES PER DAY	POUND MILES
Camel	400	25	_____
Canoe, per paddler*	500	38	_____
Donkey	100	20	_____
Human (Head-loader)	60	20	_____
Ox	200	20	_____
Ox Cart	600	20	_____

* Large canoes with up to 100 paddlers could travel about 45 miles per day downstream with the current or about 30 miles per day upstream paddling against the current. This example uses 38 miles per day as an average figure.

From *World History: Focus on Economics,* © National Council on Economic Education, New York, NY

ACTIVITY 3
TRANSPORTATION COSTS

Name _____

Using the same figures given in Activity 1, compute the approximate cost for several of these methods of transportation. Exact cost data is not available for all transportation methods, but some costs can be estimated from other information.

FACT: Camels cost about five times as much as donkeys. Assume a value of $5 for each camel and $1 for each donkey.

FACT: One driver was needed for every four camels.

FACT: One driver was needed for every five donkeys.

FACT: Some hired workers received about $.07 per day in wages.

Assume that a cargo of 8,000 pounds had to be transported 500 miles. What would be the total cost for a camel caravan? For a donkey caravan?

How much would the same trip cost if head-loaders were used?

LESSON FOUR
HOW DID THE BLACK DEATH RAISE LIVING STANDARDS IN EUROPE?

INTRODUCTION

History In the middle 1300s, Europe experienced one of its most severe natural disasters: the Black Death. A combination of bubonic and pneumonic plagues, the Black Death appeared in Europe in 1347. It started in Constantinople and Sicily, spread through the Mediterranean, then invaded northern and western Europe in 1348 and 1349. By 1350, the Black Death had killed approximately one-third of the people of Europe, with mortality rates approaching 70 percent in some locations. Later visitations of the plague in the 1360s killed up to 20 percent of the survivors and their children.

Mystery How could a natural disaster like the Black Death lead to better lives for European peasants?

Economic History Before the Black Death, the population of Western Europe had grown so much that it was difficult to feed everyone using the agricultural methods available then. Feeding that many people forced most people to work in agriculture, and tied them closely to the land and the medieval landlord-serf system.

While the Black Death killed about one-third of the people of Europe, it did not affect the amount of land and other natural resources available. By increasing the amount of land per person, the Black Death made serfs much more valuable to landlords, allowing the serfs to gain increased independence and eventual freedom from the feudal system. The increase in the amount of land per person also made it profitable for landowners to use more land for grazing sheep, leading to more wool production, which in turn led to a shift in employment from farming to manufacturing woolen goods.

CONCEPTS
Choice
Incentive
Production Costs
Profit

OBJECTIVES
◆ Calculate the effects of a reduced labor supply on the profitable uses of land

◆ Understand how the population decrease caused by the Black Death affected the economic freedom of laborers and helped lead to the emancipation of serfs from the feudal system

LESSON DESCRIPTION
The teacher displays a visual showing information on the effects of the Black Death in Europe. Students then read two short passages describing the relationship of landlord and serf in England in the years before and after the Black Death and examine these differences in class discussion. Working in small groups, students take the role of a landlord and determine the most profitable use of labor before and after the Black Death.

TIME REQUIRED
One class period

MATERIALS
1 transparency of Visual 1
■ 1 copy of Activities 1 and 2 for each student

PROCEDURE
1. Introduce the lesson by reminding students that events in history have effects not only when they happen but also in later years, particularly if the event changes society's institutional arrangements. Even natural disasters like the Black Death can affect the course of history in ways that create future benefits for society.

2. Display Visual 1 to introduce students to the Black Death and relate the material in the visual to coverage of the Black Death in the students' world history textbook.

3. Distribute copies of Activity 1. Have the students read the activity, then discuss the materials. Focus the discussion initially on identifying

★ all students–basic course material
■ average and above average students

the differences in the peasant-lord relationship before and after the Black Death, especially the change in the peasants' obligations from days of labor to money payments. Ask students to consider which system provides more incentives for peasants to work harder, produce more, and try to find better methods of farming. (The money rent system provides more incentives, because the peasant farmer personally gains from any increase in output.)

4. Distribute Activity 2. Have students working in small groups take the role of an English lord deciding how to use his land for growing food or grazing sheep, before and after the Black Death. Have students answer questions 1 and 2 in Case 1, making sure they have the correct answers (550 acres to feed lord and peasants, 450 available for market production.), then give them a few minutes to talk in their groups about how to find the answers to question 3. Point out that the lord wants to use all land for something worthwhile, and have all 15 peasants doing useful work.

5. After allowing students to think about question 3, suggest that they use a "trial and error" approach to answering the question:

A. Start by putting all available land into food production (450 acres in Case 1).

B. See whether there are enough peasants to produce food on that much land; each peasant can only work 30 acres of land. (There are 15 peasants, so there are just enough peasants to produce food on 450 acres in Case 1.)

C. Calculate how much income the lord would receive from this use of land and peasants. (£30. Each of the 15 peasants produces £2 from 30 acres.)

D. Try moving one peasant, and 150 acres of land, from food production to wool production. Does this increase or decrease your income as lord? (This would leave 300 acres, require 10 peasants to be involved in food production, and generate £20 in income from food. The 150 acres and one peasant involved in sheep grazing would

generate £5, for a total of £25. There would be four peasants with nothing to do. The lord is better off keeping all 450 acres in food production.)

6. Have students answer question 4 for Case 1. (Having another peasant family would cost the lord £2, and would gain him nothing; he has no unused land, so he would have to take 30 acres from food production for the market to feed the new peasant family.)

7. Have students go through the same procedures for Case 2:

A. Now only 400 acres are needed to feed the residents, leaving 600 acres for market production.

B. Assigning all 600 acres to food production creates a problem with wasted resources: there are only 10 peasants, so only 300 acres can be used effectively for food production, generating £20 in income, and leaving 300 acres unused.

C. Moving one peasant from food production to sheep grazing leaves nine peasants raising food on 270 acres of land, generating £18 of income, and one peasant grazing sheep on 150 acres of land, generating £5 of income, for a total income of £23; there are still 180 acres of land unused. Since £23 income is better than £20 income, it is worthwhile for the lord to have at least one peasant grazing sheep now, after the Black Death has reduced the number of peasants.

D. Moving another peasant from food production to sheep grazing leaves eight peasants raising food on 240 acres of land, generating £16 of income, and two peasants grazing sheep on 300 acres of land, generating £10 of income, for a total income of £26; there are still 60 acres of land unused. Since £26 income is better than £23 income, it is worthwhile for the lord to have at least two peasants grazing sheep.

E. Moving a third peasant from food production to sheep grazing would result in three peasants grazing sheep on 450 acres of land, generating £15 of income, and would leave 150 acres of land where five peasants could raise food, generating £10, for a total income of £25; all the land is now used, but two peasants have nothing to do. Since £26 income is better than £25 income, it is not worthwhile for the lord to have three peasants grazing sheep. Having two peasants grazing sheep is more profitable.

F. With eight peasants using 240 acres to grow food, and two peasants using 300 acres for grazing sheep, there are still 60 acres left unused. If the lord accepts another peasant family, 30 acres could be used to feed that family, and 30 more acres used for growing food for market, generating another £2 of income. The lord would be happy to have another peasant family now; it would even be worth paying a peasant family some money to move to his estate.

CLOSURE

Summarize the lesson by reviewing the changes in the relationship between the landowners (the lords) and the peasant farmers before and after the Black Death. Stress in your review the answers to question 4 in the two cases in Activity 2: what made the lords willing to give peasants more economic freedom after the Black Death was the increased value of peasant labor to the lords. Also point out that the shift to producing more wool after the Black Death would lead to more people involved in manufacturing clothing and more trade with other countries, helping to set the stage for the Industrial Revolution in later centuries.

VISUAL 1
THE BLACK DEATH IN EUROPE

- Started in Constantinople

- Spread unwittingly by trading ships

- Carried by rats and fleas

- Killed almost one-third of Europe's population, 1347–1350

- Returned several more times in the late 1300s

How did this natural disaster help lead to economic growth?

ACTIVITY 1
LORD–PEASANT RELATIONSHIPS IN ENGLAND BEFORE THE BLACK DEATH

Name _____

Most land was owned by the nobility (the lords) or by the church. Peasants did not have the freedom to move to another location. If land was sold or transferred from one lord to another, the peasants were part of the purchase.

Each peasant family had the use of 30 acres of land for growing their own food and limited use of pastureland for raising a few animals. The same 30 acres were handed down to the peasant's sons, generation after generation. The fields were planted, cultivated, and harvested according to the plans set by the lord.

Peasants were usually required to work three days per week on the lord's farmland. During the harvesting of the lord's fields, additional work was required of all members of the peasant's family. The lord's officials supervised the work, trying to make sure that peasants worked as hard as possible.

In addition to work, the peasant owed the lord various payments at specified times during the year, such as a goose or chicken at Christmas. His daughters could not marry without payment to the lord. And when the peasant died, his family was required to give his best animal to the lord.

CHANGES FOLLOWING THE BLACK DEATH

The great decrease in the number of peasants available to work the land caused by the Black Death led to drastic changes in the relationship between lord and peasant. Conflicts between peasants wanting a better deal and lords trying to keep the old relationship intact led in England to the Peasants' Revolt of 1381. The leaders of the revolt demanded that the customary obligations of peasants be abolished in exchange for a fixed rent payment. Although the Peasants' Revolt did not succeed in 1381, over the next few decades the lords were forced to grant more freedoms to the peasants.

By the early 1400s, independent farmers producing for the market, and paying fixed money rents to the lords for the use of their land, had replaced peasants tied to the land. These farmers were free to farm their land as they chose, rather than having to follow the lord's methods. They and their children were also free to move to another lord's territory, or to move to the growing towns and cities and seek work there.

DISCUSSION QUESTIONS

1. How did the relationship of peasants to their lords change before the Black Death to after the Black Death?

2. Which system provided more incentives for peasants to work harder, produce more, and try to find better methods of farming?

Information from Douglass C. North and Robert Paul Thomas, *The Rise of the Western World*, Cambridge, and G. M. Trevelyan, *History of England: Volume 1*, Garden City, N. Y.: Doubleday & Company, Inc., 1953.

ACTIVITY 2

Name _____

You are a minor noble in England during the middle 1300s. Your have a modest estate, with 1,000 acres of farmland, a small castle, and cottages for peasant families who work your land. You can use your 1,000 acres of farmland to grow food or to graze sheep, or use some of the land for food and some for grazing sheep. You need to be sure to set aside enough land to grow food to feed you and your family and the peasant families who work for you. If you graze sheep on any leftover land, you can gain money by selling wool for weavers to make into cloth. If you grow more food than you need, you can gain money by selling the surplus to craftsmen and merchants who live in a nearby town. You have to decide how you are going to use the land before and after the coming of the Black Death.

Data (the money values are hypothetical)

• You have 1,000 acres of farmland available.

• Feeding each peasant and his family requires 30 acres of farmland.

• Feeding you and your family requires 100 acres. (You eat better food than the peasants do.)

In addition to producing food for himself, his family, and your family, each peasant can:

• Grow food for market on 30 acres of land, producing £2 of income for you, OR

• Take care of sheep grazing on 150 acres of land, producing £5 worth of wool.

CASE 1

In 1345, before the Black Death, you have 15 peasants and their families living on your estate.

1. How many acres of land do you need to feed your family and the 15 peasant families?

2. How many acres are left for producing food or wool for market?

3. How should you allocate this land between food production and sheep grazing, so that you get the most income? (You can ask you teacher for a hint on how to do this.)

    Acres of food production _____
    Income produced   _____

    Acres of sheep grazing _____
    Income produced   _____

    Total income   _____

(continued on following page)

ACTIVITY 2 (continued)

4. If a peasant from a neighboring estate wanted to move to your estate, would it be economically worthwhile to you to let him move to your estate? (Remember that it takes 30 acres of land to feed him and his family.)

CASE 2

In 1352, after the Black Death, you have only 10 peasants and their families still living on your estate; the other five peasants died from the Black Death.

1. How many acres of land do you need to feed your family and the 10 peasant families?

2. How many acres are left now for producing food or wool for market?

3. How should you allocate this land between food production and sheep grazing, so that you get the most income? (You can ask your teacher for a hint on how to do this.)

Acres of food production   _____
Income produced   _____

Acres of sheep grazing   _____
Income produced   _____

   Total income   _____

4. If a peasant from a neighboring estate wanted to move to your estate, would it be economically worthwhile to you now to let him move to your estate? After the Black Death, would it be profitable for you to **pay** a peasant to move to your land?

LESSON FIVE
WHY DIDN'T CHINA DISCOVER THE NEW WORLD?

INTRODUCTION

History In the early 1400s China was more technologically advanced than Europe. During that time, China embarked on a series of naval expeditions of much vaster scope than those of the Portuguese or Spanish at the end of the century. However, within a few years China ceased its maritime explorations.

Mystery With a chronological head start and superior technology, why didn't China, rather than Spain or Portugal, discover the New World?

Economic History Technology was important to overcoming barriers to ocean voyages, but so were the beliefs and attitudes of societies. Chinese culture did not provide the kinds of incentives that encouraged trade and exploration.

CONCEPTS
Economic Growth
Technology
Trade
Incentive

OBJECTIVES
◆ Identify several examples of technology that the Chinese possessed before the Europeans did

◆ Explain several Chinese beliefs that served as disincentives to voyages of exploration

◆ Analyze the relationship between social attitudes and economic growth

LESSON DESCRIPTION
Students in small groups discuss reasons why a nation might sponsor voyages of exploration. The teacher displays and discusses a visual showing several innovations of importance to ocean exploration that appeared in China well before they did in Europe. Students then read about a series of Chinese naval expeditions that took place from 1402 to 1433 and discuss reasons why the Chinese government did not sponsor more ocean voyages after 1433.

TIME REQUIRED
One class period

MATERIALS
1 transparency of Visual 1
★ 1 copy of Activity 1 for each student

PROCEDURE
1. Ask class to develop a list of reasons why a nation's government might support voyages of exploration. (National prestige, new territory, military advantages, additional resources, new markets for products, scientific curiosity.)

2. Ask class for a recent example of governments sponsoring voyages of exploration. (Sponsorship of space exploration by the United States and the former Soviet Union.) Ask students what they think the motives of the United States and the former Soviet Union were for sponsoring space exploration. (Answers will vary.)

3. Explain that in the 15th century most ships traveled along sea coasts. To navigate the ocean, ships had to be able to sail far away from the sight of land. They had to be strong enough and large enough to withstand ocean storms. Long voyages of discovery were difficult or impossible without certain *technological* advances. Define "technology" as the application of scientific knowledge to the solution of practical problems.

4. Display Visual 1 and explain how each of these technological achievements was useful for ocean voyages. (A rudder is a vertical blade at the stern of a vessel that can be used to change directions. Multiple sails allow a ship to sail into the wind. When a ship is damaged, watertight compartments prevent water from filling the entire hull and sinking the ship. A leeboard is a board lowered into the water to prevent a ship from drifting sideways. A magnetic compass shows direction to navigators who are out of sight of land.) Note that Columbus's ships had neither leeboards nor water-

tight hull compartments, since these innovations had not yet been introduced in Europe.

5. Suggest that there is an economic mystery about the discovery of the New World (the continents of North and South America). The Chinese had better equipment, and they had it earlier than did the nations of Europe. Why didn't Chinese explorers, rather than Portuguese and Spanish explorers, discover the New World?

6. Distribute Activity 1. Divide class into groups to read and discuss Activity 1, with one person in each group taking notes on the discussion. (Answers: The five points listed in Activity 1 were disincentives to voyages of exploration because:

A. Emperors after Yung-Lo regarded naval expeditions as too expensive, given the financial condition of the government.

B. Repelling Mongol invasions was expensive.

C. An important motive for exploration is to find profitable trade opportunities, but this motive would be dishonorable according to Neo-Confucian philosophy.

D. An explorer who was away from home on a long voyage would be unable to care properly for the tombs of his ancestors.

E. If the Chinese believed that foreign cultures and their products were inferior, they would have little incentive to learn more about, or trade with, foreign countries.)

CLOSURE

Remind students that the level of technology in ancient and medieval China was in general much higher than that of Europe. Many of the inventions that we think of as European in origin actually appeared first in China. To give just a few examples, the Chinese were making cast iron in the 4th century B.C. and steel by the 2nd century B.C. Matches were invented in the 6th century A.D. and the mechanical clock in the 8th century. Many other examples of Chinese technology can be cited, but these inventions and innovations did

not lead to persisting economic growth in China. Useful inventions were not produced in large numbers to raise the living standards of the people or to trade with other countries. The Chinese beliefs that material gain was not important, that trade was a sordid activity and that foreign cultures were inferior, did not provide the kinds of incentives that can lead to economic growth.

VISUAL 1
TECHNOLOGICAL ACHIEVEMENTS
IMPORTANT TO OCEAN VOYAGES

	CHINA	EUROPE
Axial Rudder	1st Century	12th Century
Multiple Masts and Sails	2nd Century	14th Century
Watertight Compartments in Ship Hulls	2nd Century	18th Century
Leeboard	8th Century	16th Century
Magnetic Compass (as used in navigation)	9th to 11th Centuries	12th Century

Robert Temple, *The Genius of China: 3,000 Years of Science, Discovery, and Invention*, New York: Simon and Schuster, 1986.

ACTIVITY 1
THE VOYAGES OF ZHENG HE

Name _____

Between 1405 and 1433 A.D., the Chinese government (primarily during the reign of the emperor Yung Lo, 1403-1425) sent seven naval expeditions south and west to India, Persia, Arabia, and Africa under the leadership of Zheng He. Many of these expeditions included several hundred ships and thousands of sailors and soldiers. Some of the ships employed were over 440 feet long, 180 feet wide at the broadest point, had four decks, and could carry over 1,000 men.

In contrast, when Columbus sailed from Spain in 1492, he had a fleet of only three ships. His flagship, the Santa Maria, was only 115 feet long, with a deck length of 60 feet. It was a half-decked ship and carried a maximum crew of 40. The other two ships were even smaller.

After 1433 the Chinese government launched no further naval expeditions. In 1436 the emperor forbade the building of ships for overseas voyages. Forty years later, the government destroyed the records of the voyages of Zheng He. While Spanish and Portuguese explorers claimed the lands of Central and South America, the Chinese withdrew from the seas.

Why did China not follow up on its technological superiority? Explain how each of the following statements provides reasons why the Chinese government ceased to sponsor voyages of exploration after 1433.

1. The Chinese government had an inadequate system for collecting taxes. The spending of Yung-Lo's government greatly exceeded the tax revenue that could be collected.

2. In the mid-1400s, Mongols began frequent attacks on China's north border.

3. Neo-Confucian scholars held many important government posts. Neo-Confucian philosophy advocated the suppression of desire for worldly things. Trade was held in contempt. Particularly after Yung Lo's death, the influence of the Neo-Confucian scholars grew.

4. The Chinese believed that each person had a duty to care regularly for the tombs of his ancestors.

5. Most Chinese believed that their civilization was superior to all others, that foreign goods were inferior to Chinese goods, and that there was little to be learned from foreigners.

LESSON SIX
THE DECLINE
OF SPAIN

INTRODUCTION

History In the late 1400s and early 1500s, Spanish commanders Columbus, Pizarro, and Cortez claimed lands rich in gold and silver for the Spanish crown. Between 1503 and 1650, 16 million kilograms of silver and 185,000 kilograms of gold entered the Spanish port of Seville.

Mystery In spite of the gold and silver that flowed into Spain, Spanish rulers declared bankruptcy eight times between 1557 and 1680. Living standards of the Spanish people fell and famine was common. Spain became one of the poorest nations in western Europe and even today lags behind most western European countries economically.

Economic History The Spanish economy failed to grow for many reasons. These included disastrous government spending and taxing policies, expulsion of minorities with productive skills, failure to cultivate a productive middle class, and inappropriate reactions to the inflation of the 1500s.

CONCEPTS

Economic Growth
Government Spending
Taxation
Monopoly
Human Resources
Inflation
Price Controls

OBJECTIVES

◆ Analyze the effect of government policies on economic growth in the case of 16th century Spain

◆ Develop a list of economic policies that favor economic growth

LESSON DESCRIPTION

Students work in groups to study the Spanish economy in the 16th century and draw conclusions for developing nations today.

TIME REQUIRED

One class period

MATERIALS

■ One copy for each group of Activity 1
★ Two copies for each group of Activities 2, 3, and 4

PROCEDURE

1. Explain that today students will be working together to study how nations can encourage economic growth. Ask students what they think is meant by the term "economic growth." (An increase in the total amount of goods and services available to people in a society.)

2. Remind students that in the late 1400s and early 1500s, the Spanish acquired lands in the New World that contained vast quantities of gold and silver. Between 1503 and 1650, 16 million kilograms of silver and 185,000 kilograms of gold were shipped to Spain from the New World. It would seem that such a vast treasure would have helped Spain to grow economically. Yet, Spanish rulers declared bankruptcy eight times between 1557 and 1680. High taxes caused the living standards of the Spanish people to fall and famine became common. Spain became one of the poorest nations in western Europe; even today Spain lags behind most of western Europe economically. Suggest to students that money alone is not enough to insure economic growth. Tell them that they will be studying Spain as an example of how NOT to encourage economic growth.

3. Divide students into groups of six. Explain that each group represents a committee of the United Nations. Give each group a copy of Activity 1 and allow them time to read it. Then give each group two copies of Activities 2, 3, and 4, and have each group appoint subcommittees of two students each to study one of the three activities. Ask each group to develop a list of policies that a developing nation should follow in order to encourage economic prosperity. Have the groups

list suggested policies in written form and explain why each would probably be beneficial to economic prosperity. (Suggested policies: Moderate government spending to avoid the need for heavy taxes or borrowing; taxes that affect all people equally or at least do not provide incentives for people to abandon productive activities; no monopolies to raise prices and shelter producers from the need to produce efficiently; no internal taxes on trade; no discrimination against minority groups; stable prices; no price controls to discourage production)

CLOSURE

Ask students to give examples from the passages they read of how the Spanish government made the wrong choices.

ACTIVITY 1
WELCOME TO THE UNITED NATIONS
ECONOMIC DEVELOPMENT TASK FORCE

Name _____

The Secretary General of the United Nations has appointed you to the Economic Development Task Force (EDTF). The task of the EDTF is to investigate the economic policies of nations of the past in order to offer advice to today's developing nations about the policies they should follow in order to achieve economic growth.

The EDTF will study several western and non-western nations. You have been assigned to the EDTF committee on 16th century Spain.

In the late 1400s and early 1500s, Christopher Columbus, Francisco Pizzaro, and Hernando Cortez claimed lands rich in gold and silver for the Spanish crown. Between 1503 and 1650, vast amounts of silver and gold entered the Spanish port of Seville.

However, in spite of the gold and silver that flowed into Spain, Spanish rulers declared bankruptcy eight times between 1557 and 1680. Living standards of the Spanish people began to fall and famine was common. Spain became one of the poorest nations in western Europe and even today lags behind most western European countries economically. Why was money not enough to assure economic growth in Spain?

Your committee will be divided into three subcommittees. Each subcommittee will study some aspects of the Spanish economy in the 16th century and develop some recommendations for nations that are trying to increase economic prosperity in the 20th century.

ACTIVITY 2
SUBCOMMITTEE ON INFLATION AND PRICES

Name_____

What is inflation? Inflation is an increase in the average price of goods and services. When prices rise, the purchasing power of money falls. Inflation typically results from infusion of a large increase in the stock of money available in a country. Since money is used to buy products, if the amount of money in circulation increases, but the number of products available to buy does not, prices will increase. People who have more money than they had before will compete for available products by paying more for them.

In 16th century Europe, gold and silver were money. As more and more gold and silver entered Spain, prices rose. From the beginning of the 1500s to the end, the average price level increased by over 300 percent. At most times, wages rose less quickly than prices, causing great hardship to already poor workers and landless peasants.

Increases in the price of grain caused special complaints, since grain was used to feed livestock and bread was an important part of the diet of the poor. In answer to these complaints, the Spanish king in 1539 imposed a maximum price for grain. Since prices of other goods continued to rise, landowners stopped raising grain and started using their land to produce other goods, such as grapes for wine. Soon there were serious grain shortages throughout Spain.

Forty percent of the gold and silver that entered Spain was claimed by the king, who sent it to other European countries to repay debts, to pay for wars, and to import luxuries that were not produced in Spain. Prices rose throughout Europe, but many European businesses prospered by exporting goods to Spain. An increase in prices can encourage the growth of businesses by increasing profits, but in this case most business growth occurred in the countries that exported to Spain.

ACTIVITY 3
SUBCOMMITTEE ON GOVERNMENT SPENDING

Name _____

The Spanish monarchs spent heavily on warfare, first to unify Spain and to drive the Moors out of Spanish territory, later, to protect the European landholdings of the Spanish Hapsburgs. Lavish spending to maintain an elegant Spanish court and to build large-scale architectural monuments also contributed to the incessant royal demand for funds.

Two devices used by the Spanish monarchy to raise money were taxation and the granting and encouragement of monopolies. Between 1470 and 1540, taxes increased by 20 times over the level from which they started. By the 16th century, the Spanish people were among the most heavily taxed in Europe. Moreover, the burden of taxation was very uneven. Ninety-seven percent of the land was owned by 2 or 3 percent of the families or by the Roman Catholic Church. The great landowners and the church were exempt from direct taxation. Thus, the tax burden fell heavily on artisans, tradesmen, and peasants. These three groups were a large part of the private economy. They produced the bread, wine, cloth, and other goods and services desired by consumers in Spain and Europe.

By the 16th century, sheep raising was controlled by a few noble families who formed an organization called the Mesta. The Spanish crown taxed the Mesta heavily, but in return granted it many favors. With the help of the government, the Mesta was able to reserve large areas of land to be used only for grazing sheep. Therefore, less land was available for raising food.

A merchant guild in the city of Burgos controlled the export of raw wool. All wool for export from whatever part of Spain had to be transported first to Burgos. Since Burgos was over 100 miles away from the nearest port, the wool then had to be hauled to Bilbao on the north coast for shipment to northern Europe.

Such monopolies raised prices of goods because lack of competition allowed the monopolists to keep prices high and protected them from the need to keep costs down by producing efficiently. They were encouraged by the Spanish crown, however, because their high monopoly profits could be taxed.

Costs were also added to goods as they traveled from one region of Spain to another. Tariffs and tolls still existed in regions that had been independent states before the unification of Spain. Although these taxes added to the cost of goods, the Spanish monarchs retained them because part of the revenue went to the crown.

ACTIVITY 4
SUBCOMMITTEE ON HUMAN RESOURCES

Name _____

Perhaps the most important productive resource that any economy has is its people. People make the decisions about what goods and services should be produced and how they should be produced. People make these decisions based on *incentives.* An incentive is anything that encourages someone to take an action or to increase effort or that discourages an action or an effort.

In early modern times, many nations and city-states experienced economic growth led by merchants and producers of finished goods such as cloth. Such people were referred to as a "middle class," wealthier than peasants and laborers, but without the prestige of the aristocracy. In Spain, particularly, aristocrats had little respect for the middle class. Furthermore, the tax structure provided a powerful incentive to discourage production and trade. Wealthy members of the middle class could buy patents of nobility from the Spanish crown, always in need of money. Once a former merchant or producer had become a noble, he no longer had to pay taxes, since the nobility was exempt from taxation. Since producing and selling goods was thought to be unworthy of an aristocrat, the new noble would withdraw his money from his business and use it to purchase government bonds or a socially acceptable government office. Spanish trade and industry declined as the middle class withdrew their investments of time and money.

In the 1400s, two of the most productive groups in Spain were Jews and former Jews, called *conversos,* who had converted to Catholicism. Many *conversos,* particularly, were among the wealthiest and best educated of Spanish commoners. Many were merchants, financiers, physicians, artisans and other economically successful people.

King Ferdinand and Queen Isabella were devout Catholics. They were concerned about *conversos* who had returned to their traditional faith. Ferdinand and Isabella obtained permission from Rome to revive the Inquisition. The initial targets of the Spanish Inquisition were *conversos* who were suspected of abandoning Catholicism. The climate of fear and uncertainty created by the Inquisition led many *conversos* to emigrate, taking with them their wealth and their talents.

In 1492, the crown's policy stiffened and it was decreed that all Jews must either convert to Catholicism or leave the country. Estimates are that of the community of 200,000 Jews, 150,000 people left the country. Spain was denied the productive skills this group could offer. A similar policy was followed regarding the Muslim Moors, whose agricultural skills were important to the rich farming areas of southern Spain.

LESSON SEVEN
THE GREAT TULIP BOOM

INTRODUCTION

History The tulip was introduced into western Europe from the Middle East in the middle of the 1600s. It flourished in the Dutch climate and became a local favorite. As the popularity of tulips increased, the price of tulip bulbs soared. A single tulip bulb sold for hundreds of times the price of a pig or a sheep and a thousand times the price of a bushel of wheat.

Mystery Why would people choose to spend a fortune on a single tulip bulb?

Economic History In the Netherlands in the 1600s, there were many wealthy people with money to invest. When the value of rare tulip bulbs began to rise rapidly, people began to buy them, not to use in their own gardens, but rather because they believed they could sell them at higher prices than they paid; in other words, they were "speculating" in tulip bulbs. Eventually tulip prices rose so high that insufficient numbers of buyers were willing to buy. Those who owned tulip bulbs tried to sell them before prices fell, but when many bulbs were offered for sale at the same time, prices fell. Each succeeding reduction in price caused more people to attempt to sell the bulbs they owned, and tulip bulbs soon became all but worthless. Many who had speculated in tulip bulbs were ruined financially.

CONCEPTS

Financial Investment
Rate of Return
Risk
Speculation

OBJECTIVES

◆ Recognize that people invest in order to earn a return on their investment, and that higher rates of return are usually associated with higher risks

◆ Understand that expected demand can drive the price of a product extremely high, as people buy with the hope of reselling at a higher price, but that speculative prices can collapse either because people stop believing that the price of the product will continue to increase, causing demand to fall, or sellers liquidate their stocks, causing supply to fall

LESSON DESCRIPTION

The teacher displays a transparency comparing the prices of many goods in the 1600s in the Netherlands to prices paid for rare tulip bulbs during the Great Tulip Boom of the 1630s. Students perform a simulation of the boom and write a short essay expressing their personal feelings about the relationship between risk and rates of return.

TIME REQUIRED

One class period

MATERIALS

A transparency of Visual 1 and a marking pen
★ One envelope for each student. Five of the envelopes should contain one "tulip bulb" each, made from the pattern in Activity 1; the rest of the envelopes should contain seven ten-florin pieces made from the same activity sheet
★ Enough copies of Activity 2 to give one copy to each student

PROCEDURE

1. Ask students how much they would be willing to pay for a single tulip bulb. (Most tulip bulbs today sell for no more than 50 to 75 cents.) After receiving various answers, tell them that at one time, some people in the Netherlands were willing to spend their entire fortunes to purchase one or two tulip bulbs.

2. Display Visual 1. Explain that the florin was the Dutch unit of currency in the 1600s, that a "last" was approximately 80 bushels, that a "tun" was equivalent to about 2,240 pounds, and that a "hogshead" was about 63 gallons. Ask students to guess what the price of a rare tulip bulb was in Holland in the 1630s. When they have made several guesses, write "2,500 florins" on Visual 1 after "one rare tulip bulb." Tell students

that in the 17th century some Dutch people spent their entire fortunes to purchase one or two bulbs. Ask students why people might be willing to spend so much money in a way that seems foolish. (As the price of tulips rose, people bought bulbs because they believed they could sell them for more than they paid. In other words, they *speculated*.) Explain to students that a *speculator* is one who buys some commodity, not to use it, but rather because he or she believes that the commodity can be sold for a higher price. Speculators often make a great deal of money, but they also risk losing a lot of money. Explain that risk is often associated with a high *rate of return*. (A rate of return is the percentage earned on investment.) For example, today most savings deposits in banks and thrift institutions are insured against loss, but they usually pay lower rates of return than do stocks and bonds.

3. Ask students what they think eventually happened to the price of tulip bulbs in the 1630s. Students will probably answer that the price fell at some point. If this answer is given, ask students to explain why the price fell. (Speculators stopped buying and tried to sell when they felt the price would go no higher.) Tell students that they are going to act as speculators themselves, to see what happened to the price of tulips.

4. Designate one student to record prices on the chalkboard. Distribute envelopes containing either a tulip bulb or seven ten-florin pieces to the other students. Explain to students that they are speculators who want to buy tulip bulbs in order to resell them at higher prices. When the simulation ends, students who currently hold the tulip bulbs will receive 2 extra credit points for each bulb, while the three students with the greatest number of florins will receive 5 points each. Explain that you will allow at least 15 minutes for buying and selling bulbs. After that, the simulation may end at any time. The best way to earn a lot of florins in this simulation probably is to buy tulip bulbs and then sell them for higher prices, but there is a risk that at some point people will stop wanting to buy bulbs or will be willing to buy them only at lower prices. Also explain to students that, whenever someone *sells* a bulb, he or she must report to the recorder the price that was paid. (Buyers should not also report

prices, as this would result in double-counting each transaction.)

5. As students begin to buy and sell among themselves, the recorder should write each price that is paid on the chalkboard. Announce the time when 5 minutes have passed, when 10 minutes have passed, and when 15 minutes have passed. Have the recorder make a special mark on the chalkboard beside the last price recorded before each time announcement. Allow the simulation to continue for a time, and then end it.

6. Give 5 extra credit points to the three students with the most florins and 2 points for each tulip bulb that a student has. Point out that the students with the greatest number of florins took a speculative risk by buying the bulbs, but that it paid off for them when they were able to sell them at higher prices. Ask students who have bulbs whether they were satisfied with a small gain (two extra credit points), or whether they would rather have sold their bulbs in hope of making more money.

7. Examine the prices recorded on the board. Have students analyze the prices paid to see if they can determine a pattern. (Ideally, prices will rise early in the game and fall as the game nears its end.)

CLOSURE

Explain that some people like to invest their money only in very safe ways, while others are willing to put at least some money in investments that are riskier but pay a high rate of return. Distribute Activity 2 and ask each student to write a paragraph or two explaining his or her answer.

VISUAL 1
PRICES OF VARIOUS ITEMS IN
THE NETHERLANDS IN THE 1630s

<u>Florins</u>

Four Lasts of Rye.................................558

Four Fat Oxen 480

Two Lasts of Wheat.............................448

Eight Fat Swine.................................240

Two Tuns of Butter 192

Twelve Fat Sheep 120

One Thousand Pounds of Cheese...............120

One Complete Bed 100

One Suit of Clothes.............................80

Two Hogsheads of Wine 70

One Silver Drinking Cup 60

One Rare Tulip Bulb ....?

Prices taken from Charles Mackay, *Memoirs of Extraordinary Popular Delusions and the Madness of Crowds*, 2nd ed., London: Office of the National Illustrated Library, 1852. Reprint, New York: Farrar, Straus and Giroux, 1932, pp. 89-97.

ACTIVITY 1

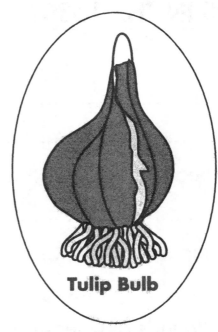

Tulip Bulb

10 Florins	10 Florins	10 Florins	10 Florins	10 Florins
10 Florins	10 Florins	10 Florins	10 Florins	10 Florins

From *World History: Focus on Economics,* © National Council on Economic Education, New York, NY

ACTIVITY 2
HOW DO YOU FEEL ABOUT RISK?

Name _____

Imagine that you are a wealthy citizen of the Netherlands in the early 1600s. You have 1,000 florins to invest. You can choose among four investments:

- Put your florins in a bank. The banker will pay you five percent interest. Bank deposits were not insured as they are in the United States today, but your banker has a good reputation, and you feel that your money is safe with him.

- Buy shares in a joint-stock company that exports goods to England and brings back English goods to be sold in the Netherlands. This venture is relatively safe, but there is a chance that the ship might sink, or that the profits of trading will be lower than expected. The joint-stock company expects to make a profit of at least 20 percent.

- Buy shares in a joint-stock company that is sending a ship to the East Indies. The journey over open seas is dangerous and the ship might very well be lost. If the venture succeeds, the joint-stock company may make a profit of three or four hundred percent.

- Buy tulip bulbs. Yesterday an acquaintance of yours sold a rare tulip bulb for 20 times what he had paid for it only a month before.

You may invest your entire 1,000 florins in one alternative, or you may divide your money among two or more investments. Write a paragraph explaining which investment(s) you chose and the reason for your choice(s).

LESSON EIGHT
ADAM SMITH AND THE MARKET ECONOMY

INTRODUCTION

History Adam Smith is often called the "father of economics" because his book, *The Wealth of Nations* (1776), gave the first systematic presentation of how the pieces of a market economy fit together, and how they operate to make efficient economic decisions. In Smith's view, the market forces of demand, supply, and price should decide what will be produced, how it will be produced, and who will consume what is produced.

Mystery According to Adam Smith, when producers of goods and services do what they think is best for themselves, they also do what is best for society, even though that was not their intention. How can people who act in their own self-interest help others?

Economic History *The Wealth of Nations* was based on the belief that buyers and sellers interacting in markets make better economic decisions than do governments about what to produce, how to produce, and for whom to produce. In the 19th and 20th centuries, this belief increasingly influenced political decisions in many nations.

CONCEPTS

Self-interest
Competition
Government Regulation
Markets
Market Economy

OBJECTIVES

◆ Understand Adam Smith's basic belief that the self-interest of producers and sellers causes them to act in ways that are beneficial to consumers

◆ Apply the concept of "self-interest" to the behavior of groups of students acting as business firms or as investors in a classroom simulation

LESSON DESCRIPTION

Students read a passage describing Adam Smith's concept of individual self-interest. Next, groups of students act as competitive producers or as investors in a simulation. Finally, they answer in writing several questions designed to debrief the simulation.

TIME REQUIRED

One class period

MATERIALS

★ 1 copy of Activities 1 and 5 for each student
★ 1 copy of Activities 2 and 3 for half of the class each
Ballots made from Activity 4 for half of the class (each ballot)

PROCEDURE

1. Distribute Activity 1 to students. After they have read it, explain that today they will explore Smith's idea that each producer in an economy, by following his or her *self-interest,* produces the goods that are most wanted by people in that society. Write the term "self-interest" on the chalkboard and ask students what they think the term means (doing something because you think that it will benefit you). Remind students of the principle of economic reasoning, "People respond to incentives in predictable ways." The hope of profit is in most cases the main incentive that guides the decisions of producers and sellers.

2. Explain that you are going to conduct a simulation in which some will act as producers and others as investors. Divide the class into two main groups, Group One, innkeepers, and Group Two, investors. Further divide Group One into three subgroups, the owners of The King's Arms Inn, The Bells and Motley Inn, or The Three Feathers Inn. Distribute copies of Activity 2 to each group. Divide Group Two into three groups, each making decisions for one potential investor. Distribute Copies of Activity 3 to each sub-group.

3. Explain to the owners of the inns that each group may choose only *one* menu to serve in their inn. Each group is to turn in to the teacher a note indicating the menu they choose and the price they will charge. (Each group should keep its

decision secret from other groups.) Later, each member of Group Two will vote on which meal he or she would choose. Before the vote, a representative from each inn will have the opportunity to make a brief sales pitch for the dinner that is being served at his or her inn.

4. Explain to each investor group that they are to choose only *one* business opportunity in which to invest 100 pounds and to report their choice in writing to the teacher. Later, each member of Group One will vote on which consumer product they would be most likely to buy. Before the vote, a representative from each investor group will have the opportunity to make a brief sales pitch for the consumer product that is being produced by his or her company.

5. After all groups have made their choices, distribute a copy of Ballot A to each student in Group Two only. Allow a representative from each inn to describe the menu that has been chosen and the price that is being charged. Suggest that each representative write the menu and price on the chalkboard. Allow students from Group B to vote, then collect the ballots and tally them on the chalkboard. Have each "inn" group calculate its profit, based on the number of dinners sold and the price charged minus the cost. Ask students whether they think any of the inns are likely to change their menus or pricing policies, based on the profit that each earned. (Probably "inn" groups that made low profits would consider either changing their menus or changing their prices. Also, if one inn's menu was highly successful, the owners might want to raise prices.)

6. Distribute copies of Ballot B to students in Group One only. Allow a representative from each investor group to make a sales pitch for the product his or her company makes. Allow students in Group One to vote, then collect the ballots and tally them on the chalkboard. Ask students from each investor group whether they think they would have made a lot of money on their investment, given the consumer preferences shown on the board.

CLOSURE

Distribute Activity 5 to each student and have them answer the questions in written form, either in groups or as individuals. (Answers: 1. Decisions about what to produce are based upon what consumers will spend money on or what producers think that consumers will spend money on. 2. Consumers may refuse to buy at all, or competitive producers may offer goods at lower prices or of better quality. 3. Investors who want to earn good returns on their money may lend funds or buy into the business, since prospects for making a profit look good.)

ACTIVITY 1
ADAM SMITH AND THE CONCEPT
OF INDIVIDUAL SELF-INTEREST

Name _____

In 18th-century Europe, the governments of most nations closely regulated the production of nonagricultural goods and services in their countries. Most European statesmen believed that government could make the best decisions about what to produce and how to produce it. For example, most nations used high *tariffs* (taxes on imports) to raise the price of foreign-made goods and discourage their citizens from buying them. Payments called *bounties* were made to domestic producers who shipped goods out of the country so that they could undersell their foreign competitors. Many imports were banned outright. Governments granted monopolies to selected individuals for producing or selling some kinds of products or trading with certain regions. The famous British East India Company, for example, had a monopoly on trade with the East Indies and India as well as on selling tea in the colonies.

In 1776, a Scottish professor of moral philosophy named Adam Smith published *The Wealth of Nations.* In this book, Smith defined the wealth of a nation as the amount of goods and services that a nation was capable of producing. Smith argued that, in most cases, government should not attempt to influence what goods were produced, how they were produced, or whether consumers bought goods from foreign or domestic producers.

In Smith's view, producers, guided by their own *self-interest,* would naturally make what people wanted most. A producer who made goods that few people wanted would probably not make much money. And as long as there was competition among sellers, suppliers motivated by the hope of profit would find it desirable to offer high quality goods at relatively low prices. Consumers would benefit most if decisions about what should be produced and sold, what prices should be charged, and so on, were made by producers and sellers trying to satisfy the demand of consumers.

The economy of the United States today follows many of the principles discussed in *The Wealth of Nations.* Our economic system is called a *modified market economy* because most of our economic decisions are made by buyers and sellers interacting in markets, although the federal government and state and local governments also make some decisions. (For example, state and local governments collect taxes to provide everyone with a low-cost public education from kindergarten through high school.) Some economists and politicians today believe that government makes too many economic decisions, while others argue that the government should provide some important goods or services for all citizens.

ACTIVITY 2

Name_____

It is the late 1700s in England. Your group owns a London inn which offers meals for sale to the public. You may choose to offer one (and only one) of the following dinners. The cost of each dinner is given. It's up to you to decide on the price. Your profit on the sale of dinners may be considered as the difference between the cost of the dinner and the price paid multiplied by the number of dinners you sell. Your alternatives are:

Mutton, cheese, mushrooms, walnuts, tarts and pickles @ 8 pence

Broiled chicken, fish, oysters, mince pie and jelly (jelly was similar to today's gelatin desserts) @ 1 shilling and 2 pence

Roast beef, apple pudding, potatoes, celery and trout @ 1 shilling

Cold ham, chicken, lobster, tarts, anchovies and cheese @ 1 shilling and 4 pence

Naturally, you want to make money on the dinners you sell. In order to do this, try to pick the dinner which you think most people would find desirable and also a price that people will be willing to pay for that dinner. Remember that a high price can bring you a good profit, but only if a lot of people are willing to pay that price.

Note: In the English money system of the time, one shilling was equal to 12 pence (pennies).

Menus and prices based on information from H. D. Traill and J. S. Mann, *Social England: A Record of the Progress of the People,* New York: G. P. Putnam's Sons, 1909.

ACTIVITY 3

Name _____

It is the late 1700s in England. You have inherited 100 pounds and would like to start your own business or buy into an already existing business. You know that you will make the best profit if you make a good that a lot of people are willing and able to buy.

Below are four possibilities for investing your money in a business:

A. Umbrellas, first introduced to England early in this century, are becoming increasingly popular. For a long time, men thought only women should carry umbrellas, but more and more men are now willing to be seen in public with one. A business that produced relatively inexpensive umbrellas so that poorer people could afford to buy one would probably be quite successful.

B. Fine china dishes were once found only on the tables of the wealthy. Ordinary people made do with wooden plates or pewter dishes. Now, new methods of production have made it possible for china dishes to be produced relatively cheaply.

C. An acquaintance of yours has developed a new recipe for tooth powder. He claims that his powder will strengthen teeth and gums so that those who use it will not lose their teeth as they grow older. His recipe consists of four ounces of powdered coral, 8 ounces of Armenian tobacco, one ounce of Portugal snuff, one ounce of Havana snuff, one ounce of tobacco ash, and one ounce of myrrh, mixed together and sifted twice. He would like you to finance a company to produce this tooth powder.*

D. More and more people are buying cotton cloth since technological advances have reduced prices. People can afford to have several changes of clothes now, and cotton, unlike woolen cloth, can be washed easily. With 100 pounds, you could buy a partnership in one of the many English factories that produce cotton textiles.

Select *one* of the business opportunities described as a place to invest your 100 pounds.

---

* This recipe taken from J.B. Botsford, *English Society in the Eighteenth Century*, New York: The Macmillan Company, 1924.

ACTIVITY 4

BALLOT A

At which inn would you be most likely to have dinner?

_____ The Kings Arms

_____ The Bells and Motley

_____ The Three Feathers

(To be given to Group Two)

BALLOT B

If you could afford to buy each of the products below and didn't currently own any of them, which would be your *first* choice:

_____ an umbrella

_____ china dishes

_____ tooth powder

_____ cotton cloth to make a garment

(To be given to Group One)

ACTIVITY 5
HOW DOES SELF-INTEREST ENCOURAGE PRODUCERS AND INVESTORS TO MAKE ECONOMIC DECISIONS THAT ARE GOOD FOR CONSUMERS?

Name _____

1. Economists often say that "consumers vote with their dollars." How does this statement apply to the simulation performed in class?

2. When sellers are offering products that many people are eager to buy, what prevents them from charging very high prices or from selling products of poor quality?

3. When a product becomes extremely popular, producers usually want to produce more than they did before. In order to do this, they have to have more money so that they can buy more raw materials, hire more workers, and perhaps even buy more capital goods. Under these circumstances, why might a producer who did not have adequate funds to expand find it relatively easy to get additional money?

LESSON NINE
THE INDUSTRIAL REVOLUTION

INTRODUCTION

History The Industrial Revolution, usually dated as starting in the middle 1700s, marked the beginning of the relatively rapid and sustained economic growth that eventually led to the current high living standards of the West, and other industrialized countries. The Industrial Revolution was primarily a British phenomenon during its early years; other countries initially lagged far behind Britain in discovering and taking advantage of new industrial technologies.

Mystery Why did the Industrial Revolution first take hold in Britain, despite some apparent advantages of other countries such as France?

Economic History For a new invention to create economic growth, the invention must become known to potential users and then actually put into use. Putting a new invention to use usually requires substantial investment, creating risks for the entrepreneurs involved. The political and economic systems that had evolved in Britain during the centuries before the Industrial Revolution created many more incentives to look for and adopt new inventions and technologies than did the political and economic systems of other countries such as France; the British systems also reduced risks that the government would take action to prevent the use of new technologies.

CONCEPTS

Incentives
Profit
Innovation
Economic Growth

OBJECTIVES

◆ Recognize several political and economic factors conducive to innovation

◆ Analyze why the British political and eco-

nomic system of the late 1700s created more incentives for innovation than did the French political and economic system of that era

LESSON DESCRIPTION

Students read an introduction to the economic aspects of the Industrial Revolution, then work in small groups to develop lists of factors that encourage innovation. After class discussion of the lists, students analyze descriptions of the political and economic systems of Britain and France during the 1700s to determine why the Industrial Revolution first began in Britain rather than France. During class discussion, the ideas developed in the lesson are applied to one or two current economic policy issues.

TIME REQUIRED

One class period

MATERIALS

1 transparency of Visual 1
■ 1 copy of Activities 1 and 2 for each student

PROCEDURE

1. List on the board some of the inventions associated with the Industrial Revolution: the spinning jenny, mechanical weaving loom, steam engine, production of wrought iron, and so on. Ask students to discuss what changes in society would be caused by these and other inventions. Ask them to think about what conditions in society would encourage people to develop and start using new inventions.

2. Distribute Activity 1 to student groups and have them complete the activity and then discuss their answers in class. Some suggested incentives might be patent protection and good education for future workers. Some disincentives might be high taxes and time-consuming and costly government regulations.

3. After some discussion, display Visual 1, and explain the factors listed to students:

A. Large number of potential customers for a product: There are usually economies of scale in industrial production; that is the cost to produce a unit of output drops as

★ all students–basic course material
■ average and above average students

the number of units produced increases. A larger number of customers for a product can help a product experience economies of scale, allowing the price to decrease.

B. Educated labor force available to produce product: Producing technological products requires workers to have sufficient education to know what they are doing.

C. Low taxes on profits: Lower taxes allow entrepreneurs to keep a larger share of profits produced. This creates an incentive to assume the risks of investing.

D. Few government restrictions on putting a new product on the market: Government restrictions can make it more costly, or even impossible, to produce a new product.

E. Patent protection from copycats: Patents provide temporary protection (17 years in United States today) for a new product by preventing others from copying it and selling an identical product.

4. Distribute Activity 2 to student groups; keep Visual 1 on display. Ask students to use Visual 1 to answer the questions on Activity 2.

Answers are below.

FRANCE

_+_ Large country, both in area and population (potentially large market)

_+_ Close to trading partners (low transport costs for trade, increasing potential market size)

_–_ Internal tariffs which split France into many small, local markets (leaves actually only a set of small markets; no gain from economies of scale)

_–_ Little international trade (no gains from larger market)

_–_ King gave monopolies to individuals on producing specific products, in exchange for tax revenues; no other businesses were allowed to enter that market (difficult for innovators to enter protected markets)

_–_ King effectively controlled taxation, and could increase taxes easily (higher taxes discourage innovators and entrepreneurs from making risky investments)

_–_ Guild restrictions on competition from outsiders were supported by King, in exchange for tax revenues (difficult to enter new markets)

_–_ No patent system to protect inventions from being immediately copied (easy for copycats to take away profits from successful innovations)

ENGLAND

_–_ Relatively small country in area and population (small market)

_–_ Isolated island (higher transport costs make trade potentially more expensive)

_+_ No tariffs on trade within England (market was as large as possible within Britain, unlike France)

_+_ Large amount of trade with other countries (larger market)

_+_ King not allowed to grant monopolies on trade to individuals after 1624 (easy for innovators to enter markets and compete with existing producers)

_+_ Powerful Parliament limited actions of King, including tax increases; Parliament dominated by merchants who wanted low taxes and freedom to trade and invest (successful innovation more profitable)

_+_ Patent system gave temporary protection from copying to new inventions (made innovation more profitable)

Despite a few disadvantages, the British system provided more incentives for innovation.

CLOSURE

Choose one or two current topics from the news that relate to government actions that affect economic incentives (Possibilities include welfare reform, health care, antitrust enforcement against monopolies— whatever is "hot."). Ask students to apply the lessons learned in this unit to analyzing whether particular government policies are likely to have a positive or negative impact on economic growth. After discussion, point out that economic growth is only one of the economic and social goals of society.

VISUAL 1
SOME FACTORS ENCOURAGING INVESTMENT IN NEW PRODUCTS

- Large potential market

- Educated labor force

- Low taxes on products

- Few government restrictions

- Patent protection

ACTIVITY 1
IS IT WORTH IT TO RISK YOUR MONEY?

Name _____

Imagine that you are a business person in the late 1700s or early 1800s. You have some savings available for investment. Think about what might encourage you to risk investing your savings in a new technology, rather than leaving your savings in a bank to earn interest. Which two of the inventions listed on the chalkboard do you think would be the most profitable investments?

INVENTIONS:

1. _____

2. _____

What government policies might provide additional incentives for you to risk investing in these new technologies? What government policies might discourage you from investing?

ACTIVITY 2
FRANCE AND ENGLAND IN THE 1700s*

Name_____

FRANCE

___ Large country, both in area and population

___ Close to trading partners

___ Internal tariffs (taxes on trade among regions) which split France into many small, local markets

___ Little international trade

___ King gave monopolies to individuals on producing specific products, in exchange for tax revenues; no other businesses were allowed to enter that market

___ King effectively controlled taxation, and could increase taxes easily

___ Guild restrictions on competition from outsiders were supported by King, in exchange for tax revenues

___ No patent system to protect inventions from being immediately copied

ENGLAND

___ Relatively small country in area and population

___ Isolated island

___ No tariffs on trade within Britain

___ Large amount of trade with other countries

___ King not allowed to grant monopolies on trade to individuals after 1624

___ Powerful Parliament limited actions of King, including tax increases; Parliament dominated by merchants who wanted low taxes and freedom to trade and invest

___ Patent system gave temporary protection from copying to new inventions

Decide whether each characteristic had a positive or negative influence on promoting the Industrial Revolution in each country. Mark the positive influences with a "**+**" and the negative influences with a "**–**". Which country's economic and political system was most positive toward promoting the Industrial Revolution?

* Based on information taken from Douglass C. North and Robert Paul Thomas, *The Rise of the Western World*, Cambridge, U.K.: Cambridge University Press, 1973.

LESSON TEN
HOW THE INDUSTRIAL REVOLUTION RAISED LIVING STANDARDS

INTRODUCTION

History Throughout the history of the world, the majority of people in most societies lived in poverty. In England in the late 1700s, significant changes in the way goods were produced increased the output of many goods and lowered costs. Lower-cost goods led to lower prices which over time resulted in a higher standard of living for people.

Mystery How can workers produce more products without working longer hours?

Economic History Josiah Wedgwood's pottery factory is used as a case study of the Industrial Revolution. The factory employed extensive *specialization* and *division of labor* to increase productivity. Wedgwood also pioneered in shifting from water to steam as a power source, and he backed the building of the Mersey to Trent Canal, which greatly lowered the costs of transporting goods to faraway markets.

CONCEPTS
Productivity
Unit Costs
Specialization and Division of Labor
Capital Goods
Technology
Transportation Costs
Standard of Living

OBJECTIVES
◆ Discover how specialization and division of labor and improved capital goods increase productivity and lower unit costs of production

◆ Identify examples of various ways of increasing productivity

LESSON DESCRIPTION
The teacher conducts a brief simulation that illustrates how specialization and division of labor and improvements in capital goods increase productivity. The teacher displays a visual that shows other sources of increases in productivity. Students work in groups to find examples of different ways of increasing productivity in a reading about Josiah Wedgwood and the Industrial Revolution and how it affected the pottery industry.

MATERIALS
Two pairs of small, blunt-edged scissors and one pair of large, sharp-edged scissors
Four red crayons
★ Approximately 60 copies of Activity 1
One transparency of Visual 1
★ One copy for each student of Activity 2

PROCEDURE
1. Remind students that, throughout the historical periods they have studied in this course, a few individuals were extremely wealthy, but most people had a very low standard of living compared to the people in today's economically advanced nations. Explain that the Industrial Revolution that took place in England in the latter part of the 18th century was important because people learned how to increase greatly the output of many kinds of goods and lower the costs of producing them. As a result, more goods became available at lower prices.

2. Write the term "productivity" on the chalkboard. Define "productivity" as an increase in the quantity of goods that a resource (such as a worker) can produce over some time period.

3. Move two desks to the front of the room. Ask two students to sit at the desks and give each a copy of Activity 1, a pair of small, blunt-edged scissors, and a red crayon. Explain that the pattern on Activity 1 is a china plate. Each of them is to cut out the china plate, color the heart red, and pass it on to the teacher, who will then give them another sheet with a plate on it. Each should attempt to complete as many plates as possible in a five minute period. Ask a student who has a watch with a second hand to start and stop the workers. At the end of five minutes, count the total number of plates that have been completed by the two workers. Inform students that you are

★ all students–basic course material
■ average and above average students

paying each worker $5. Ask them to calculate the labor cost of each plate. (Divide $10 by the total number of plates produced.)

4. Now ask the two students to specialize, one in cutting the plates out and the second in coloring. Again allow them to make plates for five minutes. At the end of this time, they should have produced more plates than before. Ask students to explain this. (Workers do not have to waste effort going back and forth between tasks.) Again calculate the labor cost of each plate. If more plates have been produced, the labor cost of each plate will be lower. Explain to students that the two workers can make more plates in the same amount of time because they have used *division of labor*—each worker specializes in doing only part of a task.

5. Now give the worker who is doing the cutting a large, sharp scissors to replace the blunt scissors. Tell this worker to cut through three pieces of paper at a time. Call up two more workers and give each a red crayon. (There should now be a total of four workers, one to cut and three to color.) Again time the workers for five minutes. The cutter should cut three plates at once and give one to each worker with a crayon. At the end of five minutes, a significantly larger number of plates should have been produced. Calculate the labor cost of each plate by dividing $20 (4 workers X $5.00) by the total number of plates produced. Emphasize that labor cost per plate has again fallen, this time because the first worker has a better scissors that can cut through three pieces of paper at once. The scissors are examples of *capital goods*—goods that are used to produce other goods. Output of plates rose this time when a better capital good was used.

6. Ask workers to return to their seats. Explain that, during the Industrial Revolution, productivity increased for many kinds of goods. That is, more goods were produced at lower unit costs. Display Visual 1, "Why Productivity Increases." Review the first two reasons, relating them to the simulation that has taken place. Discuss the other reasons. Explain that very large machines could not be operated as long as only the muscle of humans and animals was available. Machines that are operated by water power, steam power, electric power or nuclear power are more

productive than machines operated by muscle power. Explain that "technology" is the application of knowledge to producing things. Explain that the price a consumer pays for a product includes not only the cost of making that product but also the cost of transporting it from where it was made. Cheaper transportation usually results in lower prices to consumers.

7. Divide students into small groups and give each a copy of the reading, "Josiah Wedgwood and the Industrial Revolution." Ask each group to find and list examples of each kind of productivity improvement you have discussed. Also, ask them to decide what incentives they think motivated Wedgwood. (Answers: Specialization and division of labor are illustrated by the many jobs that workers had at Etruria. The steam engine illustrates better capital goods and also a better power source. Steam-powered machines to grind flint and pigment and to mix clay are also examples. Examples of improvements based on technology are illustrated by the steam-powered machinery, but also by the transfer-printing process and by Wedgwood's new clay/flint mixture. The Mersey to Trent Canal was a significant transportation improvement. Wedgwood was highly motivated by artistic considerations. He sought out the best designers and was himself a very talented artist. However, he responded to profit opportunities as well and died a wealthy man.)

CLOSURE

Ask each student to read the section on the Industrial Revolution in the world history textbook you are using and to list and classify as many examples as possible of the productivity improvements discussed in class.

VISUAL 1
SOME REASONS WHY PRODUCTIVITY INCREASES

- Specialization and division of labor

- More and better capital goods

- Better energy sources

- Better technology

- Better transportation

ACTIVITY 1

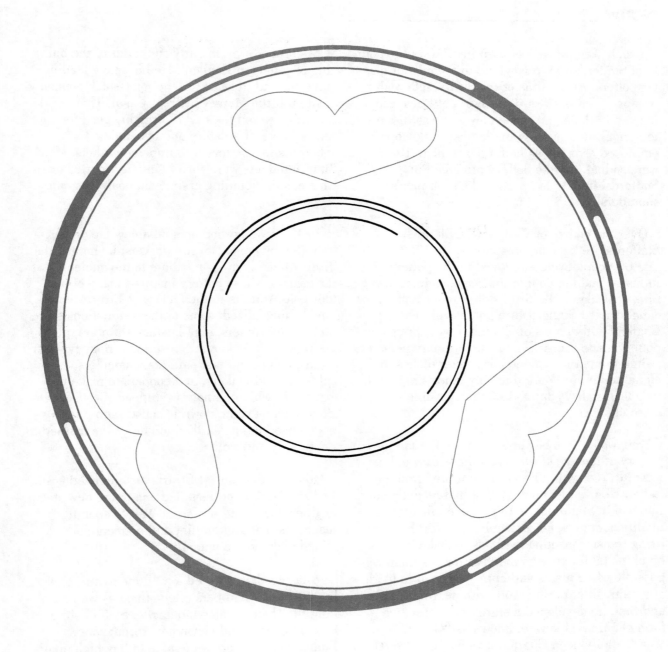

ACTIVITY 2
JOSIAH WEDGWOOD AND
THE INDUSTRIAL REVOLUTION

Name _____

Josiah Wedgwood was born in 1730 in the county of Staffordshire in England to a family of master potters. At the time of his birth, Staffordshire was poor and backward. Several potteries were located in the area, whose clay soil was ill-suited to agriculture, but only the largest workshops employed as many as half a dozen men. Roads were so bad that the pottery produced in Staffordshire had to be carried out on men's shoulders.

Over the course of Wedgwood's lifetime, Staffordshire became prosperous. By 1787, 20,000 people were employed in the pottery industry, making double the wages paid at the time of Wedgwood's birth. Better roads and a new canal carried Staffordshire pottery all over England and to most of Europe. Lower prices for pottery made it possible for the ordinary person to switch from crude wooden or pewter dishes to china tableware. More than any other single individual, Josiah Wedgwood was responsible for these changes.

Wedgwood, who began working in the family pottery at the age of nine, set himself up in business in 1759 with 20 pounds inherited from his father. He used technology that had recently come into use in Staffordshire to produce low-cost, high quality ceramics. For example, by 1760 he was using transfer printing methods to make designs on china tableware at a much lower cost than was possible when plates and cups had been individually painted. Experimenting with mixtures of clay and flint, he developed a sturdy and attractive form of china tableware, known as "Queen's Ware" after Queen Charlotte, wife of George III, accepted a set in 1762. He also produced numerous decorative items such as vases, figurines, and medallions.

Wedgwood was an early supporter of the building of canals in England. He became a leading investor and treasurer in the joint-stock company that built the Mersey to Trent Canal. This canal greatly lowered the cost of bringing good foreign clays into Staffordshire and of sending Staffordshire pottery to European markets. Many other products were soon being transported on this canal, including grain, salt, coal, iron, and copper.

In 1769 Wedgwood opened a new factory surrounded by homes for his workers; he named the little village Etruria in tribute to the ancient Etruscans, whose pottery inspired many of his designs. Workers in the factory at Etruria were highly specialized: some of the occupations there were flint-grinders, clay-beaters, throwers, plate makers, dish makers, firemen for various types of ovens, color-grinders, painters, enamelers, gilders, mold makers, and coopers to make the barrels in which china was shipped. Costs of producing china came down because each person specialized in one skill which he or she learned to do quickly and well.

Other innovations at Etruria also reduced costs. In 1782 Wedgwood installed one of the new steam engines developed by James Watt to operate machines that ground flint and pigment and mixed clay more efficiently.

Josiah Wedgwood died a wealthy man in 1795, but his efforts had benefitted others as well as himself. The ceramics industry of Staffordshire had prospered, and consumers throughout England and Europe were able to buy high quality china and other kinds of ceramics at low prices.

LESSON ELEVEN
JAPAN'S ECONOMIC MIRACLE

INTRODUCTION

History Prior to World War II, Japan was not as economically advanced as the United States, Canada, or most of the nations of Western Europe. Japan suffered heavy damage during World War II and was defeated by the United States. However, in following decades, Japan's economy grew more rapidly than did those of any of the nations that won the war.

Mystery How could Japan, whose manufacturing economy was almost completely destroyed after World War II, become one of the world's economic leaders by the mid-1960s?

Economic History Some of the things that are important to economic growth are modern capital, sufficient savings available for investment, and an educated work force. With the help of American financial aid, Japanese industries acquired modern capital. The Japanese rate of savings increased greatly in the decades following World War II, and the Japanese government had to spend very little on defense. Finally, the Japanese had a highly educated work force.

CONCEPTS

Economic Growth
Productivity
Capital
Human Capital
Interest Rates

OBJECTIVES

◆ Become familiar with increases in capital and improvements in human capital as sources of economic growth

◆ Analyze the relationship between historical facts about Japan and the rapid economic growth of Japan after World War II

LESSON DESCRIPTION

Students are introduced to a mystery about Japan's economic growth. They read a passage about economic growth and take part in a group discussion of how several facts of Japanese history are related to Japan's economic growth after World War II.

TIME REQUIRED

One class period

MATERIALS

One transparency of Visual 1
■ One copy for each student of Activities 1 and 2

PROCEDURE

1. Explain that the phrase "Economic Miracle" is often used to describe Japan's economy in the years following World War II. Ask students what they think this term means. (At the end of World War II, Japan's economy was in ruins, but by 1965 it had the third largest economy in the world, surpassed only by the United States and the Soviet Union.)

2. Display Visual 1. *(Note: After World War II, Japan lost Taiwan, Korea, and southern Sakhalin, all of which were part of the Japanese empire prior to the war.)* Ask students to suggest some reasons for Japan's rapid economic growth in the years following World War II.

3. After taking several suggestions, divide the class into separate discussion groups and distribute copies of Activity 1. Give students 5 minutes to read it.

4. Distribute Activity 2. Ask students to read it and to discuss how each of the examples helped stimulate Japan's economic growth in the decades after World War II. Select one student in each group to record the group's opinions about each explanation of Japan's economic growth. (Answers: 1. An educated work force was available in the Japanese economy after World War II; 2. Food kept workers healthy, fertilizer raised farm output, and petroleum products and industrial materials could be used to make products; 3. The Japanese government did not spend money on defense; this kept taxes relatively low, which

gave consumers more to spend and save, which provided funds for business firms to invest in ways that increased productivity; 4. Low interest rates made it less costly for Japanese business firms to invest in more machinery and equipment.

CLOSURE

Remind students that Germany was also defeated in World War II and that its economy also recovered quickly. Ask students to list some similarities and differences between Japan and Germany after World War II. (Similarities: Both lost territory; both suffered great destruction of industrial capital; both were occupied by the United States for a number of years; both had educated work forces; both received financial assistance from the United States in rebuilding their economies; the military capabilities of both were severely limited by treaty. Differences: The average standard of living in Germany was relatively high before World War II; Japan's economy is now larger than Germany's.)

VISUAL 1
JAPAN IN 1945 HAD LOST

- Almost half of its 1930 land area

- Nearly three million people

- One-fifth of its industrial plant and equipment

- Nine-tenths of its merchant marine

- One-fourth of its housing

ACTIVITY 1
ECONOMIC GROWTH

Name _____

What do we mean by economic growth? One meaning is that a nation acquires more productive resources—more labor or more land, for example. Japan expanded before World War II when it conquered new territories. Economic historians refer to this kind of economic growth as "extensive growth."

But a more important kind of economic growth is expanding the amount of output that workers can produce every day. If many workers in a nation are able to produce more goods or services every day, there are more products available for all the people in the nation. The average standard of living rises. This kind of growth is called "intensive growth." Japan experienced intensive growth before World War II, but it increased dramatically in the decades after World War II.

Let's take as an example a single worker who is producing one pair of shoes in a day. If somehow that worker can produce two pairs of shoes in a day, his or her output (the number of shoes that can be produced in some period of time, such as a day) will have doubled. Economists call such an increase an improvement in *productivity*. And if every worker who produces shoes can double his or her output, there will be a lot more shoes available at lower costs and prices.

What are some of the ways that a worker's output can be increased?

- Better tools and machinery can help workers make things faster. (Economists classify tools and machinery as *capital*—goods that are used to produce other goods or services.)

- Education and training can help workers do complicated jobs more efficiently. (Economists regard education as one source of *human capital;* educated workers are more productive.)

In a modern nation, money is usually needed to acquire capital equipment or the productive resources needed to educate people. Economists say that producers *invest* when they buy capital and when they train their workers. Governments and individuals *invest in human capital* when they pay for education or training.

ACTIVITY 2
JAPAN'S ECONOMIC MIRACLE

Name _____

The modernization of Japan's economy started long before 1945. When the emperor Meiji took power in 1867, the Japanese government began an ambitious program of economic growth and development. In the decade before World War II, the Japanese economy was growing at an average rate of 5 percent a year, one of the highest growth rates in the world. But it was still economically backward compared to the United States, Canada, and most of Western Europe.

Japan's economy was in ruins after World War II. However, in the decades after the war, the Japanese economy grew much faster than the economies of the nations that won the war. By the mid-1960s, the Japanese Gross Domestic Product (GDP) was the third largest in the world, after the United States and the Soviet Union.

Here are some explanations for Japan's economic "miracle." Why would each of the following stimulate economic growth?

1. The Japanese work force prior to World War II was highly educated, with many workers who had technical and managerial skills. Output per worker was low, however, relative to Europe, the United States, and Canada, because most Japanese factories lacked modern machinery and equipment.

2. During the American occupation of Japan (1945-1952), the Japanese received approximately $2 billion in aid from the United States in the form of food, fertilizer, petroleum products, and industrial materials.

3. The Japanese constitution, adopted in 1947, stated that Japan would not maintain its own military forces. It was understood by the Japanese that the United States would provide military protection if necessary.

4. The percentage of their income that Japanese families saved increased rapidly between 1950 and 1960. Because extensive savings were available in Japanese banks, business firms could borrow money at a low rate of interest.

LESSON TWELVE
THE FALL OF COMMUNISM

INTRODUCTION

History In the mid-1980s, over 1⅓ billion people (a little less than one-third of the world's population) were living under communist economic systems. However, by the early 1990s, almost all communist countries had begun to move away from communism and were attempting to develop market economic systems similar to those in Western Europe, Canada, and the United States.

Mystery In 1918 Russia became the first communist state. By the mid-1980s, almost a third of the world's population lived in countries with communist economic systems. But by 1990 most of these countries were in the process of changing to market economic systems. Why?

Economic History A major problem with communist economic systems was that the principle that all people in society were entitled to an equal share of the output of the society did not permit the incentive of material gain to motivate workers and producers. (In reality, there was substantial income inequality in the Soviet Union, much of it resulting from political favoritism.) Frustration with their continuously low standard of living was one of the factors that impelled citizens in many communist societies to demand major change.

CONCEPTS

Economic System
Command Economy
Market Economy
Incentives

OBJECTIVE

◆ Analyze the effects of incentives present in the Soviet communist economic system upon the performance of the Soviet economy prior to market reforms

LESSON DESCRIPTION

Students read two passages describing life in the U.S.S.R. prior to its dissolution in 1991 and, in small groups, analyze how the incentives present in the Soviet economy before the recent market reforms affected the performance of the economy.

TIME REQUIRED

One class period

MATERIALS

★ One copy for each student of Activities 1, 2, and 3

PROCEDURE

1. Explain that one of the most extraordinary changes that has taken place in recent years has been the fall of communist economic systems throughout the world. In the mid-1980s, over 1⅓ billion people lived under communist economic systems. However, today most of these countries are in the process of dismantling communist systems in favor of systems more like those of the United States, Canada and western Europe.

2. Explain that communist economic systems are based on the principles that "Each person in a society should receive an equal share of the output of goods and services that an economy produces," and "Each person should work, not for his or her personal gain, but for the good of the whole society." Ask students what they think of these principles. (Answers will vary.)

3. Explain to students that a communist system is an example of a *command economic system.* In a command economy, economic decisions are made by some authority; for example, in the Mayan civilization that existed in Mexico and Central America a thousand years ago, priests decided the three basic economic questions: "What to produce," "How to produce," and "For whom to produce." In communist countries, these economic decisions are made by the government.

4. Explain that most Western economists feel that the major problem of communist economies is that they do not provide good incentives for people to work and to produce high-quality goods and ser-

★ all students—basic course material
■ average and above average students

vices. Ask a student to define "incentive." (Answer: something desirable that encourages action or greater effort; also can be defined as things that discourage actions, such as threats of prison.)

5. Divide students into small groups. Give each student a copy of Activities 1, 2, and 3. Explain that the task of each group is to analyze how the incentives present in the economic system of the U.S.S.R. affected the output of goods and services. Have each group select a recorder to take notes on a group discussion based on the questions at the end of the reading. Students should each read, in order, Activities 1, 2, and 3, and then begin group discussion.

Suggested answers:

A. In the U.S.S.R., many goods, such as shoes and bottled water, were available only part of the time, while in the United States products that consumers want are almost always available. When a temporary shortage occurs in the United States, store owners and managers order more. In the U.S.S.R., scarce items like shoes were sometimes rationed by the government, which normally does not happen in the United States. In the U.S.S.R., workers were guaranteed employment, even if there were no need for their services or if they did a bad job. A government agency planned and built housing and decided what products factories should produce. There was a market for poor quality goods because the countries of Eastern Europe were obliged to purchase Soviet products, while in the United States nobody is forced to buy products that they consider inferior.

B. In the U.S., business firms respond to the incentive of profit by producing goods consumers want. Store owners keep products in stock so that they will not miss an opportunity to sell profitable items. Workers may lose jobs if they do poor quality work, but also have an opportunity to earn more if their efforts earn them higher pay or a promotion, or if they find a better job with a different employer.

C. Suggested changes: Allow private businesses to operate and reduce government participation in economic decision making. Stop guaranteeing jobs, but allow workers the freedom to change jobs and to decide what occupation they will follow.

CLOSURE

Reassemble the class and review answers to the discussion questions. Point out that Russia and the other now-independent states that once made up the U.S.S.R. are currently making many of the changes that the students suggested. The nations of Eastern Europe and the People's Republic of China are also introducing market reforms.

However, there are problems. For example, the former communist governments decided the prices at which goods would be sold and kept the prices low for many items that were considered necessities. These artificially low prices discouraged producers and were the cause of many of the shortages typical of communist systems. After prices were allowed to rise in accordance with supply and demand, most shortages ended, but people complained that they could not afford to buy the products available. Unemployment also became a problem in many of the former communist countries.

ACTIVITY 1
MARKET ECONOMIES AND COMMAND ECONOMIES

Name _____

An *economic system* is a set of institutions and beliefs about how economic decisions should be made in a particular society. The economic system of the United States is a *modified market economy*. In a market economic system, most decisions about what goods and services to produce, how to produce them, and who will get to use them are made by private individuals and business firms. In the United States, some economic decisions are made by our federal, state, and local governments; that's why we call our system a *modified* market economy.

In a *command* economy, economic decisions are made by some authority rather than by individuals. Until recently, the communist economy of the Union of Soviet Socialist Republics (U.S.S.R., or Soviet Union) was the best known example of a command economic system. Almost all economic decisions were made by the central government planning agency, Gosplan. All factories, farms, shops and stores, transportation and communication systems, and power sources were owned by the government. All workers were government employees.

But in the late 1980s the U.S.S.R. began to move away from a command system, introducing market institutions such as private ownership of some farmland and small businesses.

What caused this dramatic shift away from government planning? Most economists believe that a system such as the communist economy of the former Soviet Union does not provide *incentives* that encourage people to work hard and to produce high quality goods and services that consumers want at reasonable prices.

You have been given two passages written by Oklahoma economics teacher Mary Oppegard, who in 1987 escorted 28 Oklahoma high school students on a tour of the U.S.S.R, sponsored by the U.S. State Department and the Soviet government. After you have read both passages, discuss the following questions:

A. How did the Soviet economy in 1987 differ from the U.S. economy? Give examples.

B. What incentives do U.S. business firms and workers have to do a good job that were not present in the Soviet system?

C. If you were a group of advisors to the government of the U.S.S.R. in 1987, what suggestions would you make to improve the efficiency of its economy?

ACTIVITY 2
SHOPPING IN THE SOVIET UNION

Name _____

Ludmilla, our In-Tourist guide, climbed aboard our sightseeing bus, carrying a canvas bag full of heavy plastic water bottles. She picked up the microphone and apologized for being the last one to board the bus. "On the way here, I saw a line forming outside a store and joined it so that I could buy something."

She gave us tips for shopping in the Soviet Union. First, if the line was made up entirely of men, you knew that the store had a shipment of vodka. A line of women meant the store probably had clothing, especially clothing for children. "I always carry my cloth shopping bag with me," she said. "You never know when you can find a scarce item."

This time Ludmilla had obtained 10 bottles of mineral water, a desirable item in Leningrad (now St. Petersburg), where bacteria in the ancient, outmoded water system contaminated tap water. Ludmilla confided, "I have plenty of bottled water at home, but I will be able to trade this at my office for some towels that one of my friends found last week. Regardless of what the store has, I buy, so I can eventually trade for things I need."

Shopping in the Soviet Union meant standing in long lines or bartering. What Ludmilla wanted most was a pair of shoes, an especially scarce item. Her whole In-Tourist office had been allotted a quota of one pair, so they decided to draw lots for the shoe coupon. The lucky woman who drew the coupon still had to find a store with a shoe shipment. She was willing to take any size or color. Frequently only small sizes were available, because shoe factories often produced more small sizes in order to meet their production quota out of the scarce materials they received to make their shoes. Ludmilla sighed, "Shopping in the U.S.S.R. is a long, frustrating process."

The bus slowed to a stop at a tourist store. Inside the store we noticed that there were only two sales persons. Ludmilla said that she had seen one of the regular clerks at the end of the line that morning, so she probably hadn't gotten to work yet. Workers frequently missed work so that they could stand in line for goods. After all, Ludmilla explained, you couldn't be fired in the Soviet Union. We also observed that the salespeople often ignored customers. Under the guaranteed job system, no one had to worry about being fired if sales were poor.

On the other hand, workers were not able to change jobs freely or to work at the occupations they wanted. Ludmilla, for example, had wanted to be an English teacher, but government officials had decided that her excellent English skills would be better used working with tourists.

From *World History: Focus on Economics*, © National Council on Economic Education, New York, NY

ACTIVITY 3
WORKERS' LIVES IN THE SOVIET UNION

Name _____

After a long flight from Leningrad, we arrived in the middle of the night in Kishinev, the capital of Moldavia. On state-owned Aeroflot, customer satisfaction is not a consideration. No meals are served, not even peanuts or soft drinks, and flights rarely take off on time. This flight had left at 11:00 P.M., after we had waited in the foreign travelers area since 6:00 P.M.

In the eerie darkness we drove past rows of high-rise apartments on the outskirts of the city. The apartment buildings were connected to the heart of Kishinev by streetcar lines; the city resembled a wheel with spokes connecting the central city to the apartment buildings at the periphery. Kishinev suffered great destruction during World War II, and the high-rises were the solution to a massive postwar housing shortage.

Lena, our new In-Tourist guide, pointed out that many of the shops on the ground floors of the apartment buildings were empty. She said that the apartments had only two or three rooms each, with a single kitchen shared by all the occupants on the floor. Originally, the communist planners had put restaurants and cafeterias on the ground floor to encourage comrades to gather for meals together. This was cheaper than building individual kitchens. But things hadn't worked out the way the planners envisioned. Families still preferred to cook their own food and eat together in their homes, in spite of the inconvenience of sharing a kitchen down the hall.

The next day we took a bus tour to a silk factory about an hour outside the city. It was not only a factory, but also a completely self-contained city for the workers and their families—schools, day care, apartments, a clinic, stores. We were welcomed warmly by Elena, who had recently been elected as plant manager by her fellow workers. Proudly she took us on a tour. We were surprised to find only a few active workers, with many machines idle. Much of the machinery in the plant was outdated, as were the office typewriters. Because of the government's full-employment policy, many more people were employed than were actually needed. In the display room we noticed the poor quality of the finished silk fabric that was sold to Eastern bloc countries, a captive market for the U.S.S.R.

On our trip back to Kishinev, Lena pointed out a large bottling plant. She told us that the government had recently switched this plant from bottling alcoholic beverages to bottling soft drinks in an attempt to reduce liquor consumption. She laughed and said, "It hasn't slowed down liquor consumption, but it has caused a big shortage of sugar. It seems that the comrades are brewing their own!"

SAMPLE TEST QUESTIONS

Two multiple choice questions and one essay question are given for each lesson. Also note that each lesson begins with a "mystery," that can be used as an essay question. Essay questions and mysteries may be used as written test items or as small group exercises.

LESSON ONE

1. What is an "incentive"?

   ✔A. Something that encourages a person to choose or reject a particular alternative.

   B. What must be given up when a particular alternative is chosen.

   C. The result of choosing some alternative.

   D. Any choice that can be made.

2. Which of the following would probably be an incentive for a group of nomadic hunter/gatherers to adopt a settled agricultural life style?

   A. There are numerous large animals in the area in which they live.

   B. There are many kinds of wild grains and abundant nuts and berries in the area in which they live.

   ✔C. The population of their group increases so greatly that hunting and gathering no longer supply enough food.

   D. The area in which they live is warm and has abundant rainfall all year.

3. The people of ancient Sumer chose to build systems of irrigation canals. Using what you have learned about these people and their culture, explain how each of the principles of economic reasoning applies to their choice.

   1. People choose.

   2. People's choices involve costs.

   3. People respond to incentives in predictable ways.

   4. People's choices have consequences that lie in the future.

Possible Answer: This question calls upon students to use the material in their textbooks. If the text does not cover the Sumerian irrigation system, the same question might be used with a different issue, in order to give students further practice in using the principles of economic reasoning. 1) People chose to build a system of irrigation canals; 2) They had to work hard to build the canals and use time that otherwise could be used for another purpose; 3) The climate of Sumer was hot and dry, and the Tigris and Euphrates did not flood predictably, as did the Nile in Egypt. The incentive to build an irrigation system was to produce more food and to reduce the danger of crop failure if the weather was unusually dry; 4) The greater supply of food produced by irrigating (and other technological improvements related to food production) freed many workers to do other things rather than providing food. As workers specialized in other things, the standard of living rose.

LESSON TWO

1. Which of the following is an example of an increase in productivity?

    A. A Sumerian potter who usually makes three pots in a nine-hour work day stays at his shop three additional hours and makes a fourth pot.

    B. The same Sumerian potter hires a helper. Together, they make six pots in a nine-hour day.

    ✔C. The same Sumerian potter learns a quicker method of making pots, so that he can now make four pots in a nine-hour day.

    D. The same Sumerian potter makes pots of a more attractive shape that sell for more money than his old pots did.

2. Which of the following is an example of a "capital good"?

    A. A bushel of wheat.

    B. A new garment.

    C. A loaf of bread.

    ✔D. A brick oven.

3. Explain what an increase in productivity is and why it can raise living standards.

    Answer: To increase productivity means to increase the amount of output that a worker produces without increasing the amount of time that worker uses. If more goods and services can be produced without increasing the amount of labor used, a society can have more goods and services, which raises the standard of living.

LESSON THREE

1. What effect did the existence of the tsetse fly have on the trade that flourished between North Africa and the rain forest areas of West Africa?

    A. It prevented traders from bringing goods into the rain forest area.

    B. It prevented traders from using the most efficient way of transporting their goods, which was human beings carrying goods on their heads.

    C. It made it impossible for trade to take place in the rainy season.

    ✔D. It discouraged the use of donkeys and oxen in the area, even though each of these could carry more cargo less expensively than could human beings.

2. For many centuries North African merchants endured great hardships as they traveled across the Sahara Desert carrying trade goods to West Africa. What was their primary reason for doing this?

    ✔A. To make profits.

    B. To spread the Muslim religion.

    C. To obtain salt from the salt mines of the rain forest.

    D. To obtain camels from Ghana.

3. Imagine that there is a large country in which people use coal to heat their houses. Coal is produced only in the southern part of the country. In the northern part of the country, coal is quite expensive and is carried north in small trucks. Explain why each of the following would lower the cost of coal to northerners:

SAMPLE TEST QUESTIONS (continued)

1. Replacing dirt roads with paved roads.

2. Making stronger paved roads over which heavier loads can be carried without damage.

3. Building a bridge across a river that previously had to be crossed by ferry.

Answer: All of these would reduce transportation costs of carrying the coal to market. Trucks can travel more rapidly over paved roads, reducing the time needed to make the journey. Truckers would have to be paid less on a shorter journey. A stronger road would support larger trucks that carried larger loads. Trucks could cross a river faster on a bridge, without waiting for a ferry. Also, a bridge could probably bear a larger load than a ferry could.

LESSON FOUR

1. Which is true about the lives of English peasants after the Black Death had passed through England?

   A. They had less freedom than before.

   ✔B. They had more bargaining power with the lord that they worked for.

   C. Their labor was less valuable to the lord they worked for.

   D. Each peasant was less productive than previously because more peasants were required to work each acre of land.

2. The Black Death greatly reduced the population of England but did not, of course, reduce the amount of farmland available to grow food. Which of the following was then true?

   A. Because there were fewer peasants, less food was grown and many people starved.

   B. Because they did not have as many peasants working for them, the income of lords fell.

   C. Because there were fewer peasants, the income of peasants fell.

   ✔D. Because there were fewer peasants but the same amount of land, each peasant was more valuable than before to his lord.

3. In the years after the Black Death, the lives of peasant farmers changed greatly. Before the Black Death, peasants worked several days a week in the lord's field under the supervision of officials. The lord received his income from selling what the peasants produced. After the Black Death, more and more peasants became independent farmers who paid a fixed rent to the lord for use of the land. These independent farmers decided what to produce and how to produce it, and they kept the income they earned after paying all their costs, including land rent.

Do you think that peasants produced more *before* the Black Death or *after* the Black Death? Explain why, emphasizing the incentives to the peasant in each situation.

Answer: Peasants who spent most of their time producing crops to raise their lord's income would have little incentive to work hard and, working under supervision, would not be free to try to find the best and most effective farming methods. On the other hand, peasant farmers who could keep most of the income from the crops they produced would have an incentive to work hard and to try to find the most efficient ways of farming.

From *World History: Focus on Economics,* © National Council on Economic Education, New York, NY

LESSON FIVE

1. "Technology" is defined as

    A. Basic scientific research.

    B. Engineering.

    ✔C. The application of scientific knowledge to the solution of practical problems.

    D. The application of economic principles to understanding a historical situation.

2. Where were such important naval inventions and innovations as the rudder, the leeboard, the magnetic compass, multiple sails and watertight compartments in ship hulls first developed?

    A. Spain.

    ✔B. China.

    C. England.

    D. Portugal.

3. One of the most important motives for exploration is the desire for trade with other countries. Why were the leaders of China uninterested in trade until relatively recent times?

    Answer: Most Chinese believed that their own culture was superior to that of other countries and that the products of these countries were inferior to Chinese products. Also, most people trade in order to make a profit, and Neo-Confucian philosophy, which was dominant in China, taught that you should not desire the worldly possessions that profits could buy. Finally, Chinese people who went on long trade voyages could not care properly for the tombs of their ancestors, an important duty in Chinese tradition.

LESSON SIX

1. The lands that Spain acquired in Central and South America in the 1500s were rich in gold and silver, and gold and silver coins were money in Europe at that time. When large amounts of gold and silver were shipped from the Spanish colonies to Spain, what occurred?

    ✔A. Prices rose in Spain.

    B. The King of Spain became so wealthy that he reduced taxes.

    C. Prices fell in Spain.

    D. Spain began a steady course of economic growth.

2. The Spanish monarchs of the 1400s and 1500s encouraged monopolies, such as the monopoly that the city of Burgos had on exporting raw wool. Why did they do this?

    A. Because monopolies can usually produce goods and services more efficiently than competitive small producers can.

    ✔B. Because monopolies often made high profits, which the Spanish government could tax.

    C. Because monopolies usually charge lower prices than competitive small producers do.

    D. Because monopolies usually make better economic decisions about what to produce and how to produce it.

3. An incentive is something that encourages a person to choose or reject a particular alternative. In Spain in the 1400s and 1500s, why and how did each of the following Spanish government actions provide incentives that discouraged production of goods and services in Spain?

A. In 1539, the Spanish king imposed a maximum price for grain.

B. Wealthy merchants and producers could buy patents of nobility from the Spanish government.

C. In 1492, the king and queen of Spain decreed that all Jews must either convert to Catholicism or leave the country. They followed a similar policy in regard to the Muslim Moors.

Answer:

A) The maximum price for grain discouraged Spanish landowners from producing grain. They produced grapes or sheep instead. Soon there were serious grain shortages in Spain.

B) Since nobles did not have to pay taxes, there was an incentive for wealthy merchants and producers to buy their way into the nobility. And since nobles despised people who made their living by producing or selling, there was an incentive for new nobles to sell their businesses and to invest their money in government bonds or buy a government office.

C) Most Jews and Moors were unwilling to convert to Catholicism. This gave them a strong incentive to leave Spain. Since both groups were skilled in various kind of production, Spain lost many valuable human resources.

LESSON SEVEN

1. During the period of the Great Tulip Boom, Dutch buyers were willing to pay extremely high prices for rare kinds of tulip bulbs, primarily because

   A. They thought that tulips were more beautiful than any other kind of flower.

   ✔B. They thought that they could sell the bulbs for higher prices than they paid for them.

   C. They thought that, if they held on to the bulbs for 20 or 30 years, they could sell them at a large profit.

   D. They thought that beauty was more important to their lives than mere money.

2. What is the relationship between the risk of a financial investment and the "rate of return" (the percentage earned on money that is invested)?

   A. An investor can't make money on high risk investments.

   B. High risk investments usually pay a smaller rate of return than do safer investments.

   C. Risk has nothing to do with the rate of return that is earned on an investment.

   ✔D. Riskier investments usually pay a higher rate of return than safer investments do.

3. A "boom" occurs when prices in the market for some commodity or product rise rapidly. The great tulip boom of the Netherlands in the 1630s is one example of a boom, and the United States stock market boom of the late 1920s is another. Why do prices rise rapidly in such a market, and why do booms usually end with a rapid collapse of prices?

   Answer: As prices rise rapidly in a market, speculators begin to bid up prices even further because they hope to resell at higher prices. At some point in a boom, potential buyers begin to fear that prices have peaked, and they will begin to sell before prices fall. As more and more of the product or commodity is offered for sale, prices fall. Lower prices frighten other investors, who also try to sell, further lowering prices.

LESSON EIGHT

1. Adam Smith's important book, *The Wealth of Nations* (1776), described the operation of a market economy. In a market economy, economic decisions such as what to produce and how to produce are made by

    A. Government officials who set rules for markets.

    B. Business firms that have a monopoly on producing or selling some product.

    ✔C. Buyers and sellers interacting in markets.

    D. Sellers who are free to set high prices without regard to the wishes of buyers.

2. Which statement best describes Adam Smith's belief about individual self-interest?

    A. People should produce goods and services to benefit others rather than to serve their own self-interest.

    B. Governments are better judges of what economic activities are in the interests of society as a whole than are the individuals who take part in those economic activities.

    C. "Self-Interest" is just another word for selfishness. It is not right for individuals to behave selfishly.

    ✔D. When producers and sellers follow their own self-interest, they usually make and offer for sale what consumers want most.

3. Imagine that you are a maker of clocks in London in the late 1700s. You have many competitors who also make clocks. How would you best follow your own self-interest?

    Possible answer: It is in your self-interest to make as much money as possible. In order to do this, you must try to produce what people want and to satisfy your customers. You should produce an attractive clock that people would like to have in their homes. The clock should be as accurate as possible and should not break down easily. It should sell at a price that is no higher than that of similar clocks sold by your competitors.

LESSON NINE

1. In the 1700s in France, there were numerous internal tariffs on products that were transported from one region of France to another. What effect did this have on the market for French products?

    A. It encouraged producers to produce new products, since they were able to produce and sell a large number of products all over France.

    ✔B. It raised transportation costs and discouraged producers from trying to sell their products outside of small, local markets.

    C. It encouraged economic growth by raising the prices that producers received.

    D. It discouraged monopolies from forming.

2. Why were the rulers of England less able to raise taxes than were the rulers of France?

    A. English rulers understood that low taxes discourage innovation.

    B. French rulers did not understand economics as well as English rulers did.

    ✔C. The English Parliament, which contained many successful merchants and business people, had the power to raise or lower taxes.

D. The French <u>Parlement</u>, which had the power to tax, wanted high taxes to support the French army.

3. Imagine that you have an idea for constructing a housekeeping robot that will do the dishes, vacuum the rugs, wash the windows, and carry out the garbage. This could be a very popular product and make you a lot of money. However, there is a risk that you will spend a lot of time and money and not be able to develop a successful robot. How and why would each of the following government policies affect your willingness to take this risk?

A. The government allows you to take out a patent to protect you for several years from competitors copying your invention.

B. The government taxes high individual incomes heavily.

C. There is a highly educated labor force in your area, with a great many people who know a lot about science, engineering and mathematics

D. Before any new product can be brought to market, there are a great many government regulations that must be followed, and a great deal of paperwork that must be provided to government agencies.

Answer:
A) A patent allows you to sell your product at relatively high prices for a time before competition lowers it. These high prices promise you a substantial profit if you succeed.

B) High taxes on your income reduce the individual profit you might make and your incentive to take on the risk of innovation;

C) You will have a greater chance of succeeding if you can hire competent workers;

D) Regulations and paperwork add to the costs of producing and lower your potential profit.

LESSON TEN

1. When a worker can produce more units in the same amount of time, we say that his "productivity" has increased. Which of the following is NOT an example of a productivity increase.

A. Joseph is a weaver. When he first learned the trade of weaving, in the 1720s, he could produce only a small amount of cloth each day. Now that he has practiced his trade for several years, he can produce more cloth in a single day.

B. In the late 1730s, the addition of a flying shuttle to his loom doubles the amount of cloth Joseph can produce in a single day.

✔C. Joseph takes an apprentice, Ernest. Now the two of them can produce more cloth than Joseph did when he was working alone.

D. Joseph's great-grandson, William, goes to work in the 1830s in a factory which uses the power of falling water to operate looms. William's labor, aid by the powerful machinery in the factory, produces many times the amount of cloth than his great-grandfather produced a hundred years ago.

2. Which does NOT help to increase the number of products a worker can produce without increasing the amount of time he spends making them?

A. More technology.

B. Specialization.

✔C. More workers.

D. More or better capital goods.

3. What is "technology" and how do technological improvements help to reduce the cost of producing a good or service? Give two or three examples of technological improvements that occurred during the Industrial Revolution.

Answer: Technology is the application of scientific knowledge to the solution of practical problems. Some examples might be the steam engine, the power loom, canals and railroads, and so on.

LESSON ELEVEN

1. Prior to World War II, Japan was

   A. An extremely backward nation economically.

   B. A nation with one of the slowest economic growth rates in the world.

   ✔C. A nation undergoing rapid economic growth.

   D. Second only to the United States as an industrial power.

2. The term "investment in human capital means"

   ✔A. Providing education and training for present or future workers.

   B. Buying slaves.

   C. Raising living standards.

   D. Investing in business firms that employ a lot of workers.

3. Give three reasons why the Japanese economy grew so rapidly after World War II.

   Answers may be found in the lesson.

LESSON TWELVE

1. Decisions about what goods and services to produce, how to produce them, and who will receive what is produced, are made by some authority, such as a priesthood, a government, or a political party, in

   A. A traditional economy.

   ✔B. A command economy.

   C. A market economy.

   D. An orthodox economy.

2. United States high school students who visited the Soviet Union in 1987 observed that clerks in a Soviet store were not particularly attentive or helpful. What was probably the explanation of their attitude?

   A. Sales clerks were not paid at that time; they were volunteer workers.

   ✔B. At that time, workers could not normally be fired.

   C. Most sales workers were not members of the Communist party.

   D. The Soviet government at the time encouraged Soviet citizens to be rude to American travelers.

3. The economy of the Soviet Union was based to a large extent (at least in theory) upon the belief that people should work as hard as they could to benefit all the members of their society and that each person should receive an equal share of what was produced. How do you think that this belief may have contributed to a lack of economic growth in the Soviet Union in the years before the fall of Communism?

   Answer: The prospect of having a higher

income and being able to buy more goods and services is a positive incentive for workers to work hard, while the fear of losing a job is a negative incentive for hard work. Lacking either incentive, Soviet workers as a whole were not hard workers. Managers had no incentive to increase output or to produce high quality products, since doing so did not increase their income.